Y0-CPD-047

WITHDRAWN

Strangers
On
EARTH

Strangers
On
EARTH

by

Mark O'Donnell

The
Fireside
Theatre

Garden City, New York

STRANGERS ON EARTH originally appeared as a short story in Mark O'Donnell's collection, *Elementary Education* (Alfred A. Knopf, 1985). As a play, it was first produced as a workshop in January, 1989, at Whitman College in Walla–Walla, Washington, directed by Kent Paul. A subsequent workshop was produced in March, 1989, at the Seattle Repertory Theatre, Dan Sullivan, artistic director: The play was directed by Douglas Hughes.

STRANGERS ON EARTH opened in New York City on January 8, 1993, at the INTAR Theatre, produced by Zena Group Theater, Jeremy Gold and Josh Liveright, artistic directors. The play was directed by Matthew Ames, with a setting by Sean McCarthy, costumes by Kathleen Hardgrove, lighting by Amy Appleyard, and sound by Matthew Ames. The production stage manager was Michele Kay.

CAST
(in order of speaking)

HANK KNOX . . . . Jeremy Gold
PRISCILLA FAIRBURN . . . . . Elizabeth Daly
MARGARET GAMINSKI . . . . Johanna Pfaelzer
MUTT VESPUCCI . . . . Jesse Wolfe
PONY CROCKER . . . . Shaun Powell

"In this world there are only two tragedies. One is not getting what one wants and the other is getting it."

Oscar Wilde,
Lady Windermere's Fan

"Some fools don't know what's right from wrong,
But somehow, they belong.
Me, I try for all I'm worth,
But I still remain a stranger on Earth."

Feller–Ward
"Stranger on Earth"

"These all died in faith, not having received the promises, but having seen them afar off, and were persuaded of them, and embraced them, and confessed that they were strangers and pilgrims on the earth."

Hebrews 11:13

in memory of Bob Smith—
a red fox with a gold heart

CHARACTERS

HANK KNOX–26. A charismatic and talented only child, an Army brat who sometimes talks with a Texan accent to be ingratiating. He means well, but underestimates the reality of others.

PRISCILLA FAIRBURN–22. The highstrung and pale daughter of a famous WASP philanthropist, she unwittingly echoes her family charity by sleeping with men she pities; when she falls for a truly self-sufficient man (Hank), she is undone.

MARGARET GAMINSKI–22. Priss' Radcliffe roommate, a bright but rueful blue-collar prodigy from Cleveland, the youngest of a dozen. She wisecracks from a sense of the world's sadness and absurdity; a virgin, which makes her cynical.

PONY CROCKER–23. A wholesome, rambunctious and painfully repressed aspiring actor from a fatherless Mormon family; almost too 'cute.' He sings gospel music and show tunes to vent his sexual energies and exhibitionism. He's been in too many productions of *Godspell*.

MUTT VESPUCCI–35. A secretly smart layabout carpenter from South Boston. His comic tough-guy persona masks the despair of an overaged underachiever in a world ruled by money and power; his father was a small-time hood. He's sexually magnetic but intentionally gross.

The scenes of this play can be done in focused light with minimal props. The settings need not always be immediately apparent, and in fact, some degree of uncertainty about where things are happening is desirable, and in any case, the dialogue will make the place unmistakable. Just before the play begins, as the overture concludes, it may be useful to position all five characters in different places on the stage, so they can be presented "together" before we meet them individually.

ACT ONE

ACT I

SCENE 1

HANK *stands at a podium, clutching a strange trophy, a welded joke concoction bristling with symbolic ornaments—a bowler, a dog, an airplane, a lady swimmer, a winged male figure. He is beaming but hotly embarrassed, a manic, charismatic twenty-six-year-old caught up in a surprise party that is almost but not quite too much for him. He is addressing a group of his friends and his father's associates at a Houston country club. His own charming Texan accent, strangely, comes and goes as he speaks, but his aplomb and confidence carry throughout.*

HANK: Whoa! I've always had this dazed expression—and lucky for me, or unlucky for me, it's a world where that's always been appropriate! And of course my father the Possible Spy is standing here with his video camera, which merely inspires me to utter stupe-faction! Only *he* would give you a surprise party and then put you on a podium! (*He looks to his unseen father and is apparently cued to continue*) He wants a speech! (*Helplessly*) The trophy I can't explain for you, but I suspect they're mocking me because Business was my fourth major major. I'm interested in everything! And then I doubt it! First it was going to be American History, but forget that! Then I kind of cottoned to Med School, 'til I heard how they switch labels on jars of internal organs just to trip each other up! Yike! *Then* I thought Law School, but I overheard two guys in Gilley's tell the joke about the difference between a run-over skunk and a run-over lawyer—no skid marks before the lawyer? Oh, and I got briefly hepped on Architecture School, but then that hotel collapsed in Dallas! (*He grins, but instantly senses he's miscalculated*) . . . Um, I didn't mean to strike a pall just now about the hotel. I was just grasping at straws to explain this joke award . . . ! I hope none of you knew anyone involved there . . . ! (*Now back to normal*) Ouch! Anyway, this is a much happier random incident. Bla bla bla. (*He's far afield, and hopes he's sufficed, but he looks to his father and is cued to go on*) . . . I'll hope to see some of you in New York— Boo, hiss! Beat you to it!—on my boo-hiss expense account in boo-hiss public relations. (*Pause*) Well, this has *got* to be enough! Thank you for letting this Chicago hog butcher pretend to be a Texan! (*He raises a glass of champagne that was given him earlier*) I'd toast myself, but my ambition is covert! So, here's to *y'all!*

(*Blackout.*)

SCENE 2

PRISS *stands commandingly, dressed as Queen Elizabeth the First. What play is this?* PRISS *is a pale, anxious twenty-two-year-old, though it may not be immediately apparent. It's a rehearsal of a college play. She addresses a large invisible cast of her male underlings.*

PRISS: "Now, Albemarle! Now, Hastings! Come to us!
   Come, York, and all you men who serve me thus! (*She pivots confidently but strangely, as if by remote control*)
   All you, attend! My thanks, Sir Walter, friend!
   I have a great announcement to unbend.
   Recall dull Philip and his doomed armada,
   Which we reduced, to use his tongue, to *nada*—
   But now a greater challenge to our reign
   Eclipses the assaults of insect Spain.
   But be assured, I know what must be done,
   And I will shed my light like morning sun,
   And with the morning sun—for it is night,
   And midnight-uttered edicts are not right.
   Go now, most bearded friends, recede from me.

Tomorrow I will give you my decree.
And bear in mind—What I will will, will be!" (*A magnificent
pause, and suddenly her authoritative aura breaks*)
How's that? All right? I could do it again . . . Uh huh. I
see, but, Ray, may I ask something . . . ? I know you say
this is a mixture of fact and fantasy, but I'm—yes, a *factasy*,
I got that—but I'm—I'm uncomfortable, I feel like I should
just get to the point about my illegitimate baby—(*Pause. She
cringes like a child being scolded*) But why do I call them all
together just to send them all away? (*She is asked who's the
author here*) You are, Ray . . . You are, Ray. I know I'm not
the writer here. It's just . . . Maybe I should have been
Mary, the nice one who dies . . . ! All right . . . I'll try it
again . . . You are, Ray . . . Believe me, I am *trying* to be
comfortable!

(*Blackout.*)

SCENE 3

MARGARET *sits, waiting for the phone she's dialed to ring. She is
twenty-two, grimly humorous, and insistently ungroomed, if not
really plain. Beside her stands a figure of a Visible Woman, the
educational toy used to teach anatomy.*
MARGARET: . . . Hello, is this Misery Mansion? It's the Blessed
Virgin Margaret! Hi, JoAnn . . . ! Thank you for the graduation present! My own Visible Woman . . . ! No, it's amaz-
ing! It's transparent enough to be a man . . . ! Anyway, you
are one in a dozen . . . !

Yes, I know . . . I know, and I didn't expect any of
you . . .

Yes, Mom thinks travel is presumptuous . . . How *is* Miss
Havisham? Oh, I want to hear! JoAnn, nothing's so painful

that it doesn't feel better to talk about it . . . Oh, no . . .
oh, JoAnn . . . Well, can't you insist, can't you drag her to
the doctor . . . ? It's Dad who makes me furious. Why
doesn't he say something . . . ? Oh, they're such Polacks!
Peasants waiting to be run over . . . ! I know it's hard on
you, I wish Tommy would come to relieve you sometimes.
Or Ralph, or Stan, or Joey, or Bill. Don't men do sick-
beds . . . ? Where's Jane? And Nina? Or Linda . . . ?
Figures. Ungrateful kids. I just pray if I ever do have sex, I
won't conceive.

Yes, good idea, *next* . . . *!* Priss is fine. The Columbia project starts in July, if the monkey comes through. I'm in
charge of his toilet training and teaching him the subway
system. Now it can be Manhattan you all won't come to see
me in.

Uhh, she's right there . . . ? No, sure, put her on . . .
Bye, JoAnn . . . (*She now adopts a more guarded, careful,
louder voice*)

Hi Mom . . . ! You're not intruding, you never intrude,
God knows—I mean, I salute that . . . ! JoAnn says you're
having trouble breathing . . . But why shouldn't she?
Please, go to Dr. Kregar . . . ! Okay, it's a racket, but in-
dulge me, instead of a graduation present . . . ? I didn't
expect anything, I know the situation. Oh, never mind. Well,
now you've got a college grad in the brood! Are you proud
of me . . . ? Yes, I know you're proud of *all* of us, but—
What?—Goodbye? (*She holds the receiver away from herself, hurt. Her shy mother has hung up*) The mother only
love could face.

(*Blackout.*)

SCENE 4

MUTT *holds a poker hand, and sits behind a makeshift table, a board set across two sawhorses. A modest pot lies before him. He grins cagily, a boyish thirty-five-year-old from South Boston, with a comic tough-guy persona that conducts rather than reveals his true personality. He sings a South Boston fight song absent-mindedly as he appraises his hand.*

MUTT: "Here we go, Southie, here we go . . . !"

Hey, Shemp! Look alive! I got some typically bad news for you! (*He lays down his hand triumphantly*) Snicker, snicker, sneer, sneer! Poor, and I do mean poor, you! (*He rakes in the pot*) I hate to see dumb animals suffer—Why don't you leave the room? (*He grins in the other direction, to his other brother*) At least Packy knew enough to fold. He's a very *mature* thirty-eight. (*Gloats over his winnings*)—Shemp, you know why they put this little eye in the pyramid on the dollar bill? The little floating radioactive eyeball in the pyramid penthouse? I didn't think you did! It's a hypnotic eye. Sure! You didn't know that? That's what keeps us all in line, the hypnotic eye on the dollar bill. You look at it when you're buying a Hershey bar and it says: "You—love—the—American—way! You—love—the—American—way!" Sure! George Washington's state hypnotist dreamed it up. The mystic master Money. You didn't know that? And the more dollar bills you handle, the more American you get. . . . Well, yeah, quarters do the trick for *you*, cretins are fascinated by shiny objects! But that's why radicals don't believe. They don't get enough exposure to the hypnotic eye. It all has something to do with the Masons, and I don't mean bricklayers!

. . . No, thanks, I got a construction job in New York, for the Fairburns. Piece of cake, cheesecake—two Radcliffe

broads. You'll have to repossess the Monte Carlo without
me. Sorry! (*He deals a new hand. He notices some children
have approached the garage where the game is being played.
They are unseen by us, as are his brothers*) Hey, you kids!
This is a private garage! Now get out of here—or I'll saw
you into pepper steak! (*He brandishes a handy saw, and
laughs with pleasure as the children presumably flee squeal-
ing*) Ha! They love it!

(*Blackout.*)

SCENE 5

We hear cheap but friendly portable organ pep music. PONY
*stands at a microphone with a cheap, sticker-covered acoustic
guitar. He wears rainbow suspenders and a bandana with his
jeans. He is rambunctious and self-consciously wholesome, in
his early twenties but could pass for eighteen. He's concluding a
performance for an audience of school children. His playing is
passable only, though his movements are oddly suggestive for
the innocuousness of his program.*

PONY: . . . Nice playing, Mom . . . ! Once more now!—
(*sings*)

You can say, No, you know!
You can say, No, you know!
You can get through it!
I'm sure you can do it!
and who can tell how far you'll go? (*He grins, a naive version
of professional*) Well, that's all we have scheduled for the
Milk, Grain, Meat and Fruit Revue—thanks for having me at
your school! But before I go, I want to do just one more
song, a song I wrote myself, that isn't on our regular lineup.
I see your principal, Mister Booney, getting all nervous, but

there's nothing to worry about, because nobody could object
to the very simple idea in this song—even if this is a public
school—(*He strums and begins a new song, though it's ama-
teurishly similar to the one he's just finished*)
Jesus
Sees us.
Jesus
frees us!
Now here's the part
That'll touch your heart—
Jesus—
He's us!
(Do you follow this?)
Jesus—
He *is* us!

(Now this gets tricky)
Satan
Seizes us. Ouch!
Satan
Freezes us! Brr!
(Hear the difference?)
Here's some news
that I hope you can use—
Satan—
He is us!

(But luckily)
Jesus
Sees us.
Jesus
Frees us!
And here's the part
That'll touch your heart—

Jee-sus—He is us!
Jee-sus he's us!

Thank you! (*He strums a campfire chord and smiles. His gaze turns to where an angry Mr. Booney must be*) Uh, oh.

(*Blackout.*)

SCENE 6

PRISS *and* MARGARET *rush on wearing their graduation caps and gowns.* PRISS *seems to quail under a lecture from* MARGARET.

MARGARET: Honestly, sometimes I am ashamed of you!

PRISS: Please don't torture me. Margaret, I can do that for my-self.

MARGARET (*removing her gown; she wears casual clothes*): You are so wishy-washy sometimes you're in danger of drowning. How could you do that? Why did you do that?

PRISS (*following suit*): How should I know? Do you think I can read my mind? Come on! Everybody gets sudden memory blocks. Especially around their parents.

MARGARET: Lucky for you John let you off the hook and intro-duced himself.

PRISS: But we'd broken up months ago, it's not like I was keep-ing some current truth from them.

MARGARET: You'd think saying his name was like uttering the word Penis to them.

PRISS: I don't know what happened, I just was afraid my father's antennae were scanning for intruders! Even liberals are territorial!

MARGARET: And John's being black didn't enter into this the least bit? (*They begin to undress*)

PRISS (*indignantly*): Now that is a pretty low limbo. Daddy works with a lot of very tall Africans at the Foundation! Just because your family's poor, you're so proud! You think it gives you the right to criticize. (*They change quickly from jeans and pullovers to dresses suitable for dinner in a nice restaurant*) Anyhow—Nobody said a thing!

MARGARET (*in bursts, as they dress*): It was the *way* they didn't say it. It would have been Mock Around the Clock if Brother Teddy had any idea how many of Harvard's flotsam you'd been ministering to! You take the Missionary position as a whole way of life! (*Pause*) Poor little seven-foot John! (*Beat*) *There* was a romance made in Purgatory . . . ! Oh!— And Ray, the Bard of Coral Gables! That moronic Queen Elizabeth play *you* could have written better! "What I will will, will be!" . . . And, brr, whatsisname, that physicist! "Donald K. Brown, the K stands for Potassium!"—And a few others who shall remain brainless . . . !

PRISS: I never said I loved them. I just wanted to do what I could for people who needed me.

MARGARET: The mercy date! The one-woman foundation! You are a Caucasian's Caucasian! You say you want to write, but you're so full of self-denial!

PRISS: You're making me feel like a monster for trying to help people!

MARGARET: People you don't love. Tyrannized by those you pity!
Oh, what's the use of trying to talk to you? The ears have
walls!

PRISS (*hurt enough to retaliate*): . . . Even if they were just
rituals—At least I've *had* dates!

(MARGARET *is properly stung by this, which* PRISS *regrets*)

MARGARET: Speaking of low limbos . . . I'll have to have that
little pointer surgically removed. (*Pause*) Anyway, I am a tad
pickier than you.

PRISS: I'm sorry, Margaret, I know it hurts you that your family
didn't come, but you're taking it out on me unfairly. I'd expect a psychology major to have more control!

MARGARET (*sheepish*): Well . . . If I'd majored in Biology, it
wouldn't have made me immortal. (*Pause*) I'm sorry, too. We
should be thinking about the future anyway, right? (*Beat*)
Our kamikaze life pact! (*They hug briefly*)

PRISS (*trying to brighten the mood*): And more immediately,
dinner—courtesy the Fairburn Foundation.

MARGARET: Ready?

PRISS: Ready enough. (*She fastens her pearl necklace*) Am I for-
given?

MARGARET: For what, *my* bad temper? These heels make me
feel like I'm Mary getting ready for the Assumption.

(*They head out to join* PRISS' *parents and brother*)

PRISS: Margaret! what do you think tomorrow holds?

MARGARET: I don't think tomorrow holds. I think it drops.

(*Blackout.*)

SCENE 7

PRISS *sits unhappily on a pile of not-yet-unpacked boxes, facing the audience, unhappily and awkwardly smoking a cigarette and staring out an unseen window. She contemplates the street two floors below her—Upper Broadway. Paint cans or rumpled canvas may suggest the chaos of her new apartment. It's a hot summer night in early July, about nine o'clock.* PRISS *gropes for an empty paper coffee cup to use as an ashtray.* MARGARET *enters with two bags of household purchases.* MARGARET *attempts to announce her return, but a car alarm goes off outside.*
MARGARET (*over the noise*): Hi! Hello! I'm—I'm back!—(*The two women look to each other hopelessly. The alarm stops*)

PRISS: Even the machines here are hysterical!

MARGARET (*brandishing her booty*): Well—when things get tough, the tough . . . get things! (*She begins to unpack—seltzer, sponges, soap, bananas, cereal*) I've been out wandering the Eternal City.

PRISS (*pettishly correcting*): Rome is the Eternal City.

MARGARET: Well, the Endless City, then. The City That Never Sleeps.

PRISS (*glumly*): That must explain the mood it's in.

MARGARET: . . . I wish you wouldn't smoke, you look like a robot about to short-circuit.

PRISS: It makes me seem busy. If anyone were looking, they'd say, "Well, *she's* got something to do!"

MARGARET: But I expect you to be classy and highborn. Smoking is so Cleveland!

PRISS: Eek! Well, I'll put it out. I'm not sadistic, I don't want to remind you of home! (*She puts out the cigarette. Sound of hammering from other room*)

MARGARET: Mutt's still here?

PRISS: He wanted to wait 'til it cooled off to work.

MARGARET (*mimes writing*): And did you do any work today, scribble, scribble? Inward Ho!

PRISS: No. No I didn't . . . (PRISS *is not being snapped out of it by* MARGARET's *chatter*)

MARGARET: I got stamps at the post office. We live in Planetarium Station, isn't that great? Another block north and we'd be stuck in Cathedral Station! (*Beat*) I stopped by Columbia, too, but no one there knows what's going on. Dr. Spiegel's summering in the jungle—They haven't even arranged for the ape yet . . . ! Hello? What, are you anxious about your Ringer and Bellman interview tomorrow?

PRISS: I don't feel well, I think I'd better postpone it.

MARGARET: Uh oh, there's weird music on your soundtrack again. This morning the shower knobs were clenched so tight I could barely turn them on. Why so tense?—The interview is a mere formality!

PRISS (*with incongruous spirit*): All the reasons on earth can't stamp out anxiety!

MARGARET: What's that, Nervous Liberation? "I have the right to cower needlessly!"

PRISS: When you're at the mercy of others, you can't help acting like an infant! You know Mutt is taking too long on this job, and he knows it, he's toying with us! And all this moving from room to room while he's painting, it's depressing— My people are not nomadic!

MARGARET: Okay, he aspires to clodhood, but it's all bluff, and your father must have known what he's like—

PRISS: He was never like this on our summer house—(MUTT *enters with a paddle-sized piece of stray lumber. He wears wrinkled, spattered clothes, with his shirt open and untucked*)

MUTT: Hi, girls! You're looking well . . . thy! (*He completes the word 'wealthy'*) So . . . (*Examines* MARGARET's *groceries*) What're we having? (*Grinning, he fans himself with his shirt-ends, as if provocatively*) Record heat today.

MARGARET: We live in historic times.

MUTT (*enjoying the friction*): Oh Margaret, Margaret! The egghead girl in Dennis the Menace was named Margaret.

MARGARET: My, my, an allusion. (MUTT *finds and opens a bottle of seltzer*)

MUTT (*wiping his brow*): Whew! This sticky feeling, it's like that feeling you get right after you kill someone, you know? Or at least the first time you do. (*He lifts the bottle to toast*) Well, here's to sharing this place with two beautiful women! (*He drinks*)

PRISS: Mutt, you know my father did not expect you to sleep here.

MUTT: I have just one wish. Could you get a *third* woman over here?

MARGARET (*overlooking his display*): Now come on, Mutt, this makeover was supposed to take a week, not a month.

MUTT: . . . Okay, I know a couple places I can stay. I know a guy at NYU, but that'll add a lot of travelling time back and forth—

MARGARET: Let me see if I get your gambit. You act incredibly boorish so no one will expect anything from you, is that it?

MUTT (*reasonably*): It's not illegal.

MARGARET: What high standards, not illegal.

MUTT: Aww, you think I'm so low, but there's a reason. I feel obliged to be. It's fraternal, a gesture of solidarity. You'd understand if you met my brothers. If somebody says he's been low, I want to be sure I can say I understand. I'm Down There With You, Brother! (*Pause*) The bookshelves are about finished, they look good. (*Picks up the loose piece of wood*) My old man used to paddle us with a number about this size. . . . He called it the Board of Education.

MARGARET: Guess it didn't help.

MUTT: Yeah, well, I didn't go to *Hahvid* and then have my Pater hire me to re-do my place for me, but don't worry, because *I* pity *you.* I do.

MARGARET: You're a seething little self-inflicted rat bite, aren't you?

MUTT (*evenly*): At the risk of proving your point, fuck you. (*He exits into the other room*)

PRISS (*unsurely*): I don't think he meant that. (*Nervous pause*) Does he know how poor you are? That would impress him. (*Brief firecrackers outside*) Honestly, maybe I could leave til he's finished. (*Pause*) I called Squaw Creek. I could go out there for a week. It starts Monday. I told you about it, the Advanced Fiction Seminar.

MARGARET: Advanced Fiction! The only advanced fiction is the idea that you'd go there for any reason other than escape!

PRISS: Maybe I'd do some writing.

MARGARET: Maybe, maybe, the Queen of the Maybe. You at least have to stay for this job interview, your Dad went to a lot of trouble, and for Itty Bitty Bug's Sake, you're practically guaranteed the job! (MUTT *reenters, with a small duffel bag*)

MUTT: Hey, listen, I didn't mean any harm just now. We say Fuck You where I come from. Irish–Italian—We're repressed, but we yell a lot. You know how it is—We insult each other all the time so nobody ever knows when to take offense.

MARGARET: Well, Goofus plays Gallant!

PRISS: Mutt, we know you're only pretending to terrorize us.

MUTT (*laughs*): Yeah, I'm not ambitious enough for terrorism. (*He goes to door*) So . . . I'll leave my sleeping bag and stuff, and see you tomorrow. I do think you'll like those bookshelves. Women have slept with me for less. (*He leaves. The women look to each other*)

MARGARET: There are many layers to his thickness.

PRISS: He feels safe because there's two of us.

MARGARET: It's an exhibition game, like a construction worker's whistle. Compulsive because it's guaranteed hopeless. He reminds me of my brothers. Most of them, anyway.

(PRISS *lights another cigarette.* MARGARET *takes and lights one of* PRISS' *cigarettes, and draws on it thoughtfully*)

I wonder if they'll let my chimpanzee smoke. . . .

(PRISS *stares at* MARGARET *smoking*)

(*Blackout.*)

SCENE 8

PONY *reviews and revises a letter he has just written to one of his sisters. Whether or not it's obvious, he's in a YMCA room.*
PONY (*checking for errors*): "Dead"—whoops! (*He makes a correction*) "*Dear* Juicy . . . I take fingers in hand to write you this note. How are things at the Dizzy Whip? As you can

read, I must have survived the trip, unless this is my ghost writing to you! Just kidding. New York is full of honking horns, and it's not someone you know trying to say hi; and also, people reciting things to themselves on the street, and they're not all actors rehearsing, if you get the picture. They don't let you use the restrooms in McDonald's because they're afraid you're going to shoot up drugs! The very first thing I saw in Times Square was a little colored boy peeing into the street, and I thought, This Is Freedom. Or else it's Being Invisible. Hard to tell.

"I tried out for *The Ruins of Eros,* which is this play, but they said I could work props. From my window here, I can see a movie house playing *Corridors of Gore.* That'll be me someday!

"Hey—Anything can happen! but so far for me, anything hasn't.

"I hope everything has calmed down now, and again, I never thought the Jesus song was anything but cute.

"I love you in twenty-five different positions! Just kidding . . . !

"Your brother . . . , Pony." (*Pause. Now he writes a postscript*) "P.S. I want to be called Pony from now on." (*Pause. He adds another*) "P.P.S. Don't let Mom see this. I'll write her another letter without pee or drugs in it. Better burn this. Pony."

(*Blackout.*)

SCENE 9

HANK *is at his desk.* PRISS *appears as he stands and grins.*

HANK: Hi! Hank Knox! You must be Priss!

PRISS (*wincing at her nickname*): . . . I'm afraid I must!

HANK (*entertained*): Why? Do you feel sentenced to it?

PRISS (*steering away from his easy frankness*): No, no! Only to my family!

HANK: You feel sentenced to your family?

PRISS: No, I mean I'm only Priss to my family, it's one of those loving nicknames you have to put up with. I was Prissy for years! I couldn't forbid it, I was too small.

HANK: I'm sorry, I shouldn't have gate-crashed your family pet name. But your father kept referring to you as Priss on the phone. I presumed . . .

PRISS: No, I really don't mind it, I just hope people don't assume I *am* prissy . . .

HANK (*with inappropriate playfulness*): I won't! (*Awkward pause at his flirtatious note*)

PRISS (*to get over the awkwardness*): . . . Did people tease you about your nickname? Hank? Hank of hair, and pull your hair?

HANK: Interview the interviewer—Very good! No, *hank* in that sense is too obscure a word for kids. But it's not my nickname, it's my real given name, I'm Hank by law. My father wanted to convince everyone I was their pal even before they met me.

PRISS: It does sound reassuring.

HANK: Yes, if I were a cult leader, watch out! But of course I'm not. I'm too cynical for cults. Are you cynical, Priscilla?

PRISS: Er . . . Is this the job interview part? . . . No . . . I'm too idealistic to be cynical. I'm more . . . despairing.

HANK: Despair, how wholesome. I just don't care enough to give up. I'm too brittle to break. Anyway, I'm sorry Jack Ringer couldn't grill you himself, he's in the shop.

PRISS (*confused*): Like a . . . an automobile shop?

HANK: Whoops, I shouldn't joke! He's in the hospital. Nothing really. But I—Just to explain the slip—I have this fantasy belief that he has a metal electroplate, or a bit of disruptive shrapnel lodged in his skull—(*He giggles*)

PRISS (*unsure how to respond*): Maybe it's his brain that's lodged in his skull. Like everyone's, I mean. (*Pause*) He *was* injured in World War Two, wasn't he?

HANK: Well, it certainly hurt his feelings. (*Grins*) Anyway, *I* should be interviewing *you*. You *are* skilled! Now you realize this isn't quite an ambassadorship. . . .

PRISS: Yes! The Ambassador Fairburns are the other side of the family, anyhow!

HANK: You would get to receive people, though. By phone, mostly. What do you know about Ringer and Bellman?

PRISS: I know it does public relations for some very distinguished clients. It has a lot of cachet and prestige.

HANK: Yes. Cachet thanks to cash, and prestige thanks to press. You were an Economics major at Radcliffe? (*He glances at her resumé*)

PRISS: My parents' idea. I wanted to major in Psychology.

HANK: So, why didn't you?

PRISS: I don't know . . . If I did, maybe now I'd know why I didn't. (*Pause*) Eek. My roommate majored in Psychology. She said that was as close as she could get to majoring in gossip.

HANK (*helpfully*): Well, my Dad sent me to Business School, and that was more Psychology than Economics. (*Wistfully*) I once wanted to join the Peace Corps, and now here I am in the Piece of the Pie Corps. (*Beat*) Anyway, *Priscilla*. You're also a twin, pretty fascinating.

PRISS: Yes, but it's not what you're hoping! No telepathy; we're fraternal, brother and sister. It's more like a dead heat with a sibling.

HANK: And is he a good friend?

PRISS: Teddy's very patient with me!

HANK: Ah ha! You hate him!

PRISS: No, I love him, we're just different. I think puberty estranged us, embarrassed us. Something like that.

HANK: Well, that happened to me, too, and I'm an only child. . . . So did you debut and everything?

PRISS: If you're trying to make conclusions about me from that, the answer is, no. But, in fact, I didn't.

HANK: They have debutante balls in Houston, I call them Product Awareness campaigns. Bla bla bla. So, if you could have one wish at this interview, last question, what would it be?

PRISS: Well . . . I'd wish that this answer would reveal exactly what you'd hope it to.

HANK: Ah, you might as well have majored in Psychology! I'm going to flip over all the cards, Priscilla. *You've got the job.*

PRISS: Don't you have to consult your boss?

HANK: You had it all along, scarecrow, this was a mere formality!

PRISS: I'd have been hired no matter what?

HANK: Well, yes, unless you'd been truly psychotic. Mr. Ringer hates competition. Weren't you told you basically had the job?

PRISS: Yes, but I couldn't quite imagine it.

HANK: Well, you know, Priss, in this magical land, if you *have* something, you can *imagine* it.

PRISS: I did make a bet with myself that if my felt-tipped pen could stay balanced on my desk all night, I'd get the job.

HANK: What? Did it?

PRISS: No, it fell. But then I told myself not to be superstitious.

HANK: Good flip-flop! That's handy in public relations!

PRISS: Well, thanks so much! Is there anything else I need to know, or you do?

HANK: No, we have your address and phone number, and in this life isn't that all we can really know of one another? You'll start in two weeks, is that all right?

PRISS: Mm, hmm!

(*They stand and shake hands.* PRISS *goes*)

HANK (*to himself*): . . . And just for our computer records, what color are your eyes?

(*Blackout.*)

SCENE 10

MARGARET *is alone with* MUTT. *There's no more mess. He's folding up his dropcloths and he's cleaned up. She smokes, nervously maybe, but she seems languid and trusting with* MUTT.
MARGARET: Mutt. (*Pause*) But Mutt for what?

MUTT (*automatically, as he works*): Matt. Matthew Patrick Vespucci.

MARGARET: Like Amerigo Vespucci? Amerigo–as–in–America Vespucci?

MUTT: Don't say it! He got a lot of credit he didn't deserve, I agree, get off my back.

MARGARET: Mutt . . . We had a dog named Mutt. You guessed it, a mongrel. After he died, we buried him under the tree he used to like sitting under. Yes. Nice idea, but my mother started to wonder if he was facing the same direction he always liked to sit in, so the next day she had me and one of my brothers dig him up . . . ! He *was* facing in the right direction. . . . That's just typical of her. (*Pause.* MUTT *looks up*)

MUTT: I know what you could do.

MARGARET: What? (*Pause*)

MUTT: Get over it. (*Pause*) Fucked up childhood, shame on them. Fucked up adulthood, shame on you.

MARGARET: I suppose *you* jumped free of the old ancestral juggernaut?

MUTT (MUTT *snorts. An odd passion surfaces for a moment*): Huh! You Jews!

MARGARET (*this shatters the detente and pleasure* MARGARET *had been experiencing with* MUTT. *She winces*): Don't make me deny something that shouldn't matter. I'm not Jewish.

MUTT: Gaminski?

MARGARET: Polish Catholic.

MUTT (*adjusting effortlessly*): Oh. (*Beat*) You Catholics!

MARGARET (*irked*): *I'm* Catholic? *You're* the Catholic. Don't tell me that fat head of yours didn't spend some time curing in a parochial smokehouse!

MUTT: Ooo, The Cleveland Spitfire! I bet the monkeys'll go for you, the blonde–by–comparison goddess.

MARGARET: It's a chimpanzee, though I know distinctions don't bother a bigot.

MUTT: Come on, you wouldn't be playing word games with apes if you didn't want a caveman, deep in that four-chambered, trailer-home heart of yours. (*Pause*)

MARGARET: Your semen is dreamin'.

MUTT: Hey, come on! Necessity is the mother of affection.— And . . . I've got what you need!

MARGARET: Really? You're carrying a gun? (*Pause*)

MUTT: You're beautiful when you hate me. No, really, you're very sexy, you could do porno.

MARGARET: That's like saying you're strong enough to drop an anvil on your head.

MUTT: I get it, pretending to resist! I have to beat my way through a forest of thorns to get to the Beauty—

MARGARET: Oo, I hate that. Your insults are fine, it shows you respect me, it's your compliments that sting. It's galling, you're coming on to me and you know that nothing will happen. It's a compulsion.

MUTT: I'm just steering into the skid. Being what's expected. That's what personality is. (*Pause*) Anyway—I'm out of the mood now. Words are a very effective saltpeter. (*He has all his remaining equipment at the door*) I think I got everything. You can have the leftover paint. I'm moving on.

MARGARET: You are? . . . What are you going to do now? Stay in New York?

MUTT: Well, I'd accept that offer but I can stay at Larry's. Come down and see me sometime.

MARGARET: Sometime. Your passion's pretty sketchy.

MUTT: No, really. We can rent a monster movie, make smart remarks about their suffering. Women love monsters, don't they?

MARGARET: They don't have much choice. But what are you going to do for money?

MUTT: I don't know. I'd play the lottery, but I couldn't handle the math.

MARGARET: They might need some humans for a study of sleep at Columbia. I could recommend you for that. No duties, you just let them monitor your brain waves.

MUTT: Right! No thanks. I only do insane things for women I hope to go to bed with.

MARGARET (*squirming at what she's admitting*): This is so irritating. It wouldn't be so bad if you were just driven . . . to underachieve! But . . . you're secretly . . . really smart.

MUTT: Ah, now you want me! I'm losing interest. (*It seems to be a hopeless stalemate*)

MARGARET: Look, I didn't mind your pretending you wanted me. But pretending you don't? Are you trying to make me think you do?

MUTT: Well, at this point I don't even know. But it probably doesn't matter. I get the idea you were raised to be alone.

MARGARET (*stung by this*): Good-bye.

MUTT: We're parting badly. That's a good sign, isn't it? (*He goes.* MARGARET *turns away, frustrated.*

(*Blackout.*)

SCENE 11

PONY *sits on a stool with his guitar. It's an open mike night at a basement folk club.*
PONY: Hi, everybody, how you both doing tonight? What happens to be happening? I'm Pony! That's Puh—not Phuh—Ony! So don't blame me if I'm a *little horse!* (*Grins and pretends to tune his guitar*) Small world, huh? I know that's what you say when you run into people you already know, and I don't know you, so in this case—it's just an observation! But it *is* a small world, music makes it small!—Like, maybe, this song, by me? It's from my eventual first album, which I already know the title for—"Pony Express—es Himself!" Of course,

no one else knows about it yet, unless you count the desk clerk at the Y, I told him! But that's why they have Open Sesame, I mean, Open Mike Night! To be seen! Open Mike, that sounds like what they'd have to do if Michael the Archangel had cancer! (*No response follows this baffling joke*) Isn't there that story in the Bible about the dying angel who falls to earth and the innocent man killed where it lands? I may have that wrong. Well, I don't believe in patter anyway before you sing. I think you should just sing. You both look warmed up to me! No, you should just sing, that's what I say, so I will just . . . go ahead . . . and . . . heeere . . . goes!

(*He edges into his song as if into a scalding bath, but the chipper chords are very like all his other songs*)

Some men are deaf, some men are blind,
And some men can't get love off their mind!
But oh, I pity the man,
I pity the man who can!
Some smell of booze, some smell of soap,
And some men can' stop clinging to hope!
But oh, I pity the man, I pity the man who can.
(*He plays a fumbly interlude on the guitar and jokes with his audience*) Yeah, we all know it's a weird universe. But then, what do we have to compare it to? (*Singing again*)

Some men laugh, and some men cry,
And most do both an' never know why!
But one Man honestly knows—
Turn to that Man who knows!
The Man in the hat that glows!
The Man in the Bloody Clothes!
Turn to that Man who knows!

(*Conclusive chord.* PONY *grins to his unresponsive audience*)
Uh oh.

(*Blackout.*)

SCENE 12

PRISS *enters her apartment with a suitcase.*
PRISS: Hello? The place looks great! Like a photo that's developed!

(MARGARET *appears*)

MARGARET: Dickens has docked! Welcome back!

PRISS (*scanning the room*): Ah ha! *Two* dirty coffee cups in the sink! Have you crossed the border from B.C. to A.D.?

MARGARET: Calm down, Miss Marple, I'm still Before Coitus. It's two days worth of cups.

PRISS: A clean cup every day? That isn't like you.

MARGARET: I've decided adulthood means I should pamper myself.

PRISS: When did Mutt finish?

MARGARET: Last weekend. (*She writhes at the connection* PRISS *may be imagining*) It's not his cup, all right? We have the place to ourselves. Sit down. (*Seats her and herself. Mock meddlesome Yenta*) So—I wonder how your time up there was?

PRISS: Yes, so do I!

MARGARET: Was it that confusing?

PRISS: Well, I took the Short Story Intensive—

MARGARET: Did you do any writing?

PRISS: In a way. I had a fling. Strictly courtesy car. A meanwhile man. Sort of like a bomb test in the desert. No one needs to know if it misfires.

MARGARET: Some needy type? Were you the Foundation's field hospital again?

PRISS (*squirming*): Well . . . A married man. That's a rite of passage, isn't it? Being with a man who can commit—even if it's to someone else?

MARGARET: Same dead end. Upper level! What's wrong with you?

PRISS: Margaret, I didn't expect a thing from him—

MARGARET: Great, emotional necrophilia! (*Pause*) I'm sorry.

PRISS: Anyway, maybe I can use it. Out of the frying pan and into the file. What about your experiment? Has it begun?

MARGARET: No. In fact, there's trouble in Brave New Banana-land.

PRISS: Doctor Spiegel attacked by the apes?

MARGARET: In a way. He's been accused of falsifying data. Making things up.

PRISS: Oh, no!

MARGARET: Remember I told you what a big deal it was when he said his chimp Flip was learning to drive? And Flip got angry trying to learn stickshift, and made the sign for Spiegel's name and the sign for shit, he just made a connection on his own? Lorn Burks, his big rival—Spiegel's, of course —says it's all a lie, Spiegel made it up, and he's calling for a duplication of results.

PRISS: What can they do? Are they going to make Spiegel provoke the chimp at a press conference?

MARGARET: Who knows? And anyway, they could *coach* Flip, like a candidate! But that's just the first engine failing. Then the animal rights people heard about our project plan and they said to raise a chimp like a human in Manhattan would be cruel and vicious! And somehow they got in and trashed the lab *and* the simulated apartment! And now it's a big mess, so my job is on indefinite hold.

PRISS: But you haven't *lost* the job, have you? It hasn't died, it's just, like, overseas.

MARGARET: Well, it's scary, and speaking of that, I'm dreading any plumbing or heat problems—ever—because José is getting eerie in the elevator. And he isn't kidding, like Mutt was! He was clucking his tongue over whoever sprayed BIG BAD ME in the hall and I said it was probably a teenager and he started glaring at me and said, "*It is no teenager. It is someone—else.*"

PRISS: He doesn't think *you* are BIG BAD ME?

MARGARET: No, he's just punishing us, or me, for overlooking those vague sexual come-ons of his. *"It is a good day to be a man. . . ."*

PRISS: Oh, eek.

MARGARET: Well, *you* have a job, anyway. We just have to hold on.

(*Unnerved pause. These are two scared girls. Outside, we hear another car alarm*)

Is life a cruel joke, or just meaningless? I keep forgetting which.

(*Blackout.*)

SCENE 13

It's an idle afternoon at the office. Late October. HANK *hangs out at* PRISS' *reception post. He wears a faded sign, hung by string around his neck, that reads "MEN."* PRISS *wears one that reads "WOMEN."*

HANK: So, the adoption officer sips the, as it were, the coffee, and says to them, "Mmmm. I think you two would make wonderful parents."

PRISS: Oh, how could they!

HANK: They could, did, do, and will. And—it *worked* for Coffeena. The old Mouthwash–Equals–Marriage.

PRISS: My father approves of TV only when they broadcast the burning yule log at Christmas.

HANK: You're from stern stock.

PRISS (*fairly*): But, TV does give safety hints and numbers to call if you're mentally disturbed.

PONY (*entering as if to illustrate her point*): Hi! . . . I would like to see Mr. Ringer or Bellman?

PRISS (*caught relaxed, she sits up*): Oh! Hello! They aren't here today. May I help you with something?

PONY: Well, I'm willing for you to. I see in the paper you do commercials, and I wanted to drop off my photo and re-sumé.

PRISS: Well, it's actually more like consultation here. We don't do any actual casting here—.

HANK (*amused by this earnest misfit*): Have we seen you in any-thing?

PONY: Maybe you recognize me from my future stardom!

HANK: How Calvinist.

PONY: I was in *Drums Across The Land.*

HANK: I'll bet you were! What is it?

PONY: It's the biggest outdoor drama in the country! Real horses, waterfalls, real fire—.

HANK: Oh, right! Up in Utah.

PONY: I played the angel Moroni, who appears to Joseph Smith and gives him the golden tablets. They weren't real gold, but I did fly. Or was flown! I also toured in *Youth for People!*

PRISS: You did?

PONY: Well, not the *real* one, but we did the red sweaters and used the logo. It was great, but I write and perform on my own, mainly.

HANK: Well! That's great, but I think you want to go to an actors' agent. One for actors. We consult with advertisers and special groups. Or you could get into a showcase.

PONY: I did the props for the *Ruins of Eros* but you couldn't see me. It's this group called the Individual's Collective— (*Pause*) Can I leave you my picture, anyway? I was told saturation is the way! I took this course in commercials at the Knowledge Basement. You've seen the ad? "When you don't know what you're doing, go to the Knowledge Basement!"

PRISS: Er–Isn't this picture awfully small?

(*She holds up a tiny trapezoidal photo, not much more than a postage stamp*)

PONY: Yes. I'm still waiting on them, so I cut into my family photo.

HANK: How ruthless. So—(*Glancing at resumé*) Tony—

PONY: Yes, or Pony. Crocker. I made up Pony as a nickname for myself.

PRISS (*as if just meeting*): Hi. From . . . (*looks at resumé*) Hope Bluffs High!

PONY: Hope Bluffs is the desert owl capitol. It's near Salt Lake. They're actually dumb vicious creatures! Owls, I mean.

HANK: So you were a big cheese in a small trap! And now you've come east!

PONY: Yeah, I just wanted to get the time two hours sooner! (*He grins and, after all, he does have innocent charm*)

PRISS: You must miss your family!

PONY (*hopefully, to* HANK): I can't tell. It's more like I miss the friends I haven't made yet.

HANK (*reading from resumé*): Ah, *Youth for People*. Well, again, we don't really involve ourselves in casting actors, but we do work with people who sometimes do—

PONY: I really appreciate it! I can play teenage or adult.

HANK: Yes, there's a whole set of adults who play teenagers professionally.

PONY: Well, I'm there!

PRISS (*solicitously*): Do you have a job to keep you going, Pony?

PONY: Sure. At The Lost Civilization.

HANK: Right, the Aztec place. I'm Hank Knox.

PRISS: Priscilla Fairburn. Well, I wish you good luck!

PONY: I sure need it!

PRISS: Aww! (*She pats his hand. Another pity date?*)

HANK (*grinning*): "I think you two would make *wonderful* parents!"

PONY (*blushing, doesn't know it's a joke*): Aww . . . ! Anyway, thanks! You've been a great audience! Plus, I won't forget what you might do for me!

HANK: Well, don't remember too hard!

PONY: May I ask just one more question? Why are you wearing those signs?

PRISS (*she'd forgotten them*): Oh! They were being thrown out! They're redoing the washrooms down the hall, and Hank brought them in as a joke.

PONY: Ahh! Well, happy Halloween! 'Bye!

HANK: Well, 'bye.

PRISS: 'Bye!

(PONY *is gone.* PRISS *and* HANK *stare at each other*)

HANK: Wow. Pathos Bill.

PRISS: The poor thing! (*Looking at* PONY's *tiny photo*) He looks like a deer frozen by oncoming headlights!

HANK: Well, who knows, he might be great in commercials. That endearing lost look people can identify with—It's touching. I'll give his picture to Rick for the Great American Fizz.

PRISS: You're a nice person.

HANK (*teasing her*): Thanks! And I think *you're* . . . correct! No, it has less to do with my being nice than with my feeling guilty about secretly feeling sorry for him. I always do nice things for people I feel sorry for! (*Pause*) So, why don't I take you out to dinner later?

(PRISS *doesn't know whether to feel pleased or patronized. She smiles unsteadily. Blackout.*)

SCENE 14

The common room of the NYU frat where MUTT *is staying. He watches a TV whose screen is turned away from the audience. A wretched disco beat and tiny gasps are faintly heard from the TV. It's ten at night.*

MUTT (*avid, but tentative*): . . . Ooo, I'll bet this part is good, I guess! . . . (*He twists his head in several directions, as if to see better*) Oh yeah! Is that her—or him? Whoa! I wish I were seeing this . . . ! Lar', this is a fuckin' mess! If you weren't so cheap, you'd pay to get this channel!—(*Doorbell offstage*) Why don't you get it, since you're here legally and I'm not? (*Pause as* MUTT *watches TV*) Whoa, kids! Or—wait —no. That's just her in two pieces. . . .

(MARGARET *enters, momentarily unseen by* MUTT)

MARGARET: Hi!

MUTT (*panicked, unsteadily tries to cover, turns off TV*): Oh h-hi! What are you doing here?

MARGARET: Just like a man. Invites you over and then asks what you're doing there. (*She glares at the screen and* MUTT's *debasement before it*) What were you watching?

MUTT: Uhh—It's a special on Picasso's nudes.

MARGARET: It *sounded* like pornography.

MUTT (*sheepishly owns up*): Infidelity for shut-ins.

MARGARET (*icy tolerance*): Voids will be voids. Why did it look like a shattered mirror?

MUTT: It's on cable and the signal's scrambled. Larry's too cheap to pay for it.

MARGARET: I know this is a frat, but you're supposed to be an adult.

MUTT: Hey, it *said* for Mature Adults Only!

MARGARET: You must be very proud to have made the final cuts.

MUTT: Okay, already! (*Pause as they stare at each other*) You're just mad because there's no graceful way for this to be a date now.

MARGARET (*explaining her visit*): We were having trouble with our bathroom light, and I can't ask our super for help. He keeps saying things like "*Do not be afraid*" just to scare me.

MUTT: The fluorescent light? Maybe the starter needs replacing. The little silver cylinder behind the tube.

MARGARET (*flatly*): That must be it. Thanks. So long.

MUTT: Look, I know this is bad timing. But I also know this couldn't really upset you, you've worked in hospitals!—You just think you're supposed to act offended for form's sake!

MARGARET: It's depressing for me to see how awful my rivals are. A two-dimensional fragment. A torso of a ghost. What are you doing here, anyway? Half-dressed, no job, hanging out with a pack of self-made simians half your age—

MUTT: Don't underestimate the power of inertia.

MARGARET: You and your relentless one-downmanship!

MUTT (*getting angry*): Look, *you* walked in on *me!* Walk in on anyone without phoning first and you'll see the world's true shabbiness! (*Frustrated, becomes unguarded*) *You* walked in on *me!* Jesus, you know this happened before with a woman I liked. She wouldn't and wouldn't, and one night after I'd beat off *four times* thinking about her, she suddenly appears at the door!—Thanks, an after-dinner steak!

MARGARET: Doesn't the Geneva Convention forbid anecdotes like that? I can't believe I came all the way downtown just to remind myself why I hate you.

MUTT: You can't, huh? Shows what a virgin you really are.

MARGARET: If you have no more respect for me than that . . . !
(*She leaves*)

MUTT (*calling after her*): Oh, you can take it! That's what I respect! You're strong! You just don't want to *look* like you can take it! (*Pause*) Well . . . I guess that's final. . . . Again! . . .

(*He turns the TV on. The disco music sound reemerges. Blackout.*)

SCENE 15

HANK's *apartment. He sits, glazed, as* PONY *strums his guitar. A few large aluminum caterer's tubs surrounding them indicate a meal of stolen leftovers. It is after midnight.*

PONY (*with all the charm he can muster*): . . . I sang that one for this ward of suicidal patients last Christmas, in Provo . . . It felt really good. . . . It's so great to play my songs for someone really smart! I really think you're great . . . !

HANK (*automatic pilot*): Thanks, so are you! You're still idealistic. That impresses me. (*Beat*)

PONY: Are you doin' okay?

HANK (*rousing himself*): Hm? Oh, sure. All this free food has made me drowsy. I didn't think you'd be coming over so late.

PONY: I had to wait 'til they closed the party to take the leftovers.

HANK (*trapped in his kindly gesture*): Maybe I need another drink. Strictly southern logic, I know. How about you?

PONY: No, I'm fine. (*He blows bubbles through his straw to make bubbles in his bourbon and ginger ale*) Look! Frankenstein's lab!

HANK: Chilling. Will you be ready for another one, though?

PONY: Sure, though I remember reading in Ann Landers that if you order another drink before one is finished, it's a sign you're an alcoholic.

HANK: Oh, Pony—renegade Mormon! (*He mixes* PONY *another drink*) But why'd you pick Pony? I didn't think it was allowed to pick your own nickname.

PONY: I was sick of Tony. I thought Pony could be sexy or not sexy at the same time, just to be safe. (HANK *offers him a new drink*)

PONY (*hopefully; already tipsy*): Whoosh! Are you trying to get me drunk?

HANK: Nope, just compulsively hos-pitable! Trained in Texas! (PONY *takes a reckless swig from his drink*) Wow! That was quite a guzzle there! Is that how you swizzled Go, the Great American Fizz?

PONY: We were swigging it all day, I got sick! All of us in our swimsuits in the cold chugging around the Statue of Liberty! That statue is unreal! This one guy, Greg—(*Checks praising anyone besides* HANK)—And, uh, your friend Rick says he can use me in other stuff! I'm getting my card! Thanks to one You!

HANK: Rick says you went in for this Japanese robot toy they're bringing over!

PONY: Yup! Doctor Everything! He changes from a robot to a flying warrior to . . . anything! A metal dog, say! I'd be Doctor Everything's human helper! Rick just had me say, "We must capture Treasure Tower!" over an' over!

HANK: Capture Treasure Tower! Well, that's pretty basic! Phallic and Capitalist Imperative—with a catchy beat! And you'd be the token human?

PONY: I'm supposed to be an adult kids can identify with.

HANK: Saved every Saturday by a cast-iron Christ! (*He realizes his possible gaffe*) Oh, I hope that doesn't offend you!

PONY: Don't worry, you couldn't offend me!

HANK: Well, I noticed all your songs have Jesus in them. Are you born again or something?

PONY: Oh, no! I was barely born the first time! No, Jesus just goes with the music! I love gospel, it's fun to sing, it's sexy! My poor Mom—I used to perform with her—she gets all confused when I start to sing about Jesus like I was colored —(*He finishes his drink*) What . . . I do like about Jesus . . . is . . . he was a stranger on earth! He was nice, but nobody got him! Isn't that what people get into, how weird it was for Jesus, all alone?

HANK: Is it?

PONY: And people in songs always seem alone, don't they?

HANK (*dubious*): Do they?

PONY: I don't know, maybe it's the echo chamber. Can I have another drink?

HANK (*obliging*): Ask and you shall therefore be typical.

PONY: When I was like six, I remember noticing that love songs always took place at night, everyone singing in the cold and dark, and when I asked my Mom why love songs take place at night she said because people have jobs and can't get together during the day.

HANK: Very tasteful. And when did you get the real facts?

PONY: I never did! (*He laughs at his own joke, but* HANK *finds the moment weird. He hands* PONY *yet another drink. To cover,* PONY *toasts again*) Well . . . Capture Treasure Tower! (*He makes mock-explosion and laser sounds, and drinks*)

HANK: That's what my Dad expects me to do. To capture treasure tower. His expectations are like sunlight—focused through a magnifying glass—on an ant. Does your Dad have high hopes for you?

PONY: He may, I don't know. He's dead. (*Pause.* HANK *winces*) It's okay, he died when I was three, of a heart attack at work. The Mormon motto is INDUSTRY. Plus, I think he was a secret coffee drinker. I'm the only son, but I was premature. My big sisters always gave me my way, it's like I came back from the dead!

HANK: All that attention made you uncomfortable?

PONY: No, it felt too good, that's why I left. Women are too easy to please!

HANK (*almost gagging*): I don't know about that!

PONY: Who wouldn't be pleased with you?

HANK (*uneasy but deft*): Thanks.

PONY (*helpfully*): Well, I'll go! I'm drunk! (*He stands, a bit unsteadily, and when* HANK *assists him, hugs him.* PONY *quickly covers by turning his gambit into a joke. He squeezes* HANK *tightly*) "So, Mistah Bond! You fall into my trap!" (HANK *defensively squeezes back, even lifting* PONY *off the ground. Finally, as if to say "uncle,"* PONY *makes a sound like a rag doll whose stomach button has been pressed*) "Ma-Ma!" (HANK *releases him.* PONY *retrieves his guitar. Pause*) I hope we can be friends.

HANK: If that's what you mean, I hope so, too . . . ! Give my best to Doctor Everything! And all the little Everythings!

PONY: You know what? You would make a great TV talk show host.

HANK: You think so? Well . . . "Goodnight Everybody!" (PONY *gives him another last-licks hug*) Oof! Nice having you!

PONY: Nice to be had!

HANK (*tactfully breaking the hug*): Nice to see you!

PONY (*taking his guitar case in hand*): Nice to be seen!

HANK: 'Bye!

(PONY *goes.* HANK *turns back in, understanding* PONY's *loneliness and probable sexual problems*)

HANK: Uh oh.

(*Blackout.*)

SCENE 16

PRISS' *bedroom.* HANK *and* PRISS *lie in bed together. Three a.m. She looks at him uncertainly; he smiles in seeming sleep.*
PRISS (*gingerly*): Hank . . . ? Are you asleep? Hank . . . ? Tell me . . . About your last girlfriend . . . What went wrong?

HANK (*blankly, as if hypnotized*): She tried . . . to get me . . . to talk in my sleep . . . about my old girlfriends . . . That's . . . why I killed her . . . (*He grins*)

PRISS (*chastised*): Are you mocking me now, too?

HANK (*opens his eyes, sits up partially and draws her close. He pulls her cheek like a fond uncle. Pause. He improvises a dreamy nursery rhyme*): Priscilla, Priscilla,
My melting vanilla,
Paler than spilled milk . . . under the moon . . . (*He kisses her lightly*) You know what I wish for?

PRISS: Peace on Earth?

HANK: That would be cagey, wouldn't it? Good sound bite. Sure, fine. I also wish . . . for Peace on Priss.

PRISS: Me, too. I'm anxious to be peaceful.

HANK (*kisses her*): You're beautiful. You're a secret treasure, even to yourself. You know what your Dad said when he was describing you over the phone? "She surprised us all by turning out gorgeous!"

PRISS: Yes, I wish they'd concealed their surprise.

HANK (*hugs her*): Well, you have my love. Is that any help?

PRISS: Love, you fling that word around like a credit card.

HANK: Do you doubt my love, or doubt that you're lovable?

PRISS: I appreciate the encouragement, but isn't it a little too soon? Too easy?

HANK (*puzzled but trying to oblige*): Well, would it help if I said I was insincere? (*Pause*)

PRISS: Yes. (*Pause*) But you might not mean it.

HANK (*enjoying her girlish hesitation*): Ha . . . ! Love, love, the frangible intangible . . . (*Kisses her again*) It's almost three. Should I go now?

PRISS: I don't know. Is there some kind of moral equator after three a.m.? Would we be transformed?

HANK: I think I need transforming.

PRISS: No, you don't.

HANK: I don't need it?

PRISS: No, you don't think you do.

HANK: What do you mean?

PRISS: Nothing, just that you're a very confident person. After dating a lot of misfits, it's so strange to be with an ultra-fit. A one size fits all, even. Everybody likes you.

HANK: I do have a wide acquaintance. I should sell little soaps. In fact, I want to tell you about this comical job opportunity that's come up! Old Man Ringer has written a book!

PRISS: Oh, no!

HANK: A self-help book, of all things. *You Can Make Them Like You!*

PRISS: Eek. But *he* certainly can't! He's grating and driven!

HANK: Exactly. And ugly. His publisher wants a presentable co-author they can send out on the talk-show circuit.

PRISS: Co-author? You're going to *write* it with him?

HANK: It's all written! I do the front work, take the hubris and humidity off it. The reverse of a ghost-writer. I provide the person. You probably disapprove, Miss Struggling Writer.

PRISS: Who never writes anything. Well, as long as you see the humor of it.

HANK: Come on, this'll be just one more wagon for my circus train of memories. (*Beat*) I will have to tour around the country for a couple months.

PRISS: It sounds like you've already decided.

HANK: Should I have consulted you?

PRISS: Of course not. (*Pause. She sighs significantly*)

HANK: Uh oh. Remorse Code. What's the matter?

PRISS: Nothing.

HANK: That old steamroller nothing. Don't worry so much. You're being pecked by your chickens before they're hatched.

PRISS (*pause*): . . . You just don't seem to need me, really.

HANK: . . . Maybe not. But that doesn't mean I can't love you. (*He makes to engage in a love bout, but senses* PRISS *is not enthusiastic*) . . . Now what?

PRISS: I just don't want to have my heart broken.

HANK: Not that whammy! Look. I don't break hearts. Hearts don't get broken. Hearts break themselves.

(*She looks at him unsurely, but there is a lot in what he says. The lights fade out.*)

SCENE 17

PRISS *is nervously dressing for an evening with* HANK, *two weeks later. She has just dropped her hand mirror and looks to the floor with horror.* MARGARET *rushes to her.*
PRISS: He'll be here any minute!

MARGARET: Obviously. (*She watches* PRISS' *last-minute prepara-tions*) If your father knew you were going to a party in a Republican's honor, he would be horrified.

PRISS: Look. Hank wants me to meet his father. His father and Mr. Horrifying are friends. Should I have said no? I want to meet his parents.

MARGARET: The mother will be there too?

PRISS (*irked at* MARGARET's *use of* 'the'): "The" mother? No, "the" stepmother. His Dad's been married three times. Also an overachiever. (*Beat*) And talk about overachieving! When I was at Hank's last week, he brushed his teeth *while* peeing *and* humming at the same time.

MARGARET: I've been dragged behind the chariot of your ro-mances before, but this is the first time I've seen you fasci-nated.

PRISS: I *am* fascinated. He's a dreamboat.

MARGARET: Dreamboats never dock. (*Portentously*) And remem-ber, fascinating and fascist are from the same root.

PRISS: Margaret, why do you resent him? You haven't even met him yet!

MARGARET: I'm just disliking him for your sake. Your infatuation needs checks and balances. From what you say he says, it isn't really a reliable romance.

PRISS: But it could be.

MARGARET: Could be isn't is. Is is is.

PRISS: Well, it's too late. I've dived in, I can't dive out. (*The downstairs buzzer rings*) Here he is. (*She presses the front door release button*) And please, don't be offended because he's gracious. (*She is clearly anxious about* MARGARET *and* HANK *meeting*)

MARGARET: Just remember—You're the victim. That gives you the upper hand!

PRISS (*she opens the door for* HANK): Hello!

HANK (*off*): It's Big Bad Me!

PRISS: You're unforgivably prompt! (HANK *appears with a bouquet of flowers. He kisses her lightly, in deference to* MARGARET) This is Margaret, my roommate. Hank, of course.

HANK: Nice to meet you!

MARGARET: Nice to meet you! Priss has said some ultimately nice things about you!

HANK (*undeterred*): Ha! I won't mess with that one. These are for you (*He offers the flowers to* MARGARET)—since I couldn't wangle a ticket for you to the reception.

MARGARET (*stymied*): Thank you, you didn't have to do that! I'd be out of place, anyhow. The receptions I go to, firemen slide across the floor on their stomachs to win five-dollar bets.

HANK: That sounds like a lot more fun than this sorry *soirée*.

PRISS: Do we need to go right away?

HANK: Well, it's hip to arrive late. If we were really hip we wouldn't go at all.

MARGARET: Hip Republicans! This modern world. (*Awkward moment*) Priss says you're going on a book tour!

HANK: Yes, for a book I co-authored but haven't read! And you're doing volunteer work, tutoring? That's great.

MARGARET: Well, until this research job comes through, I might as well be righteously unpaid.

HANK: We who make hefty salaries salute you! (*The doorbell rings again*) Are you expecting someone?

PRISS: No . . . (*She goes to open door, leaving* MARGARET *and* HANK *awkwardly alone*)

MARGARET: So . . . You're from Texas or something?

HANK: Or something. I just pretend to be Texan. People like it. (*He turns his gaze to the door.*) It's a bike messenger! (MUTT *appears in a cyclist's helmet, bike tights, and windbreaker.* PRISS *follows, secretly pleased he's visiting* MARGARET)

MUTT: I was in the neighborhood on a run, I thought I'd see how the place is settling in. Looks good!

PRISS: Hank, this is Mutt—er—Matt Vespucci, he did the painting and carpentry here when we moved in. This is Hank Knox.

MUTT: Oh, right! The Ringer and Bellman boy! I deliver packages up there all the time.

Priss (Elizabeth Daly), Pony (Shaun Powell) and Hank (Jeremy Gold)
in the 1993 Zena Group Theater production at the Intar Theatre,
New York City, "high comedy in a gentler vein…charming and wise."
—Michael Feingold, *The Village Voice*

Photos by Bill Kavanah

Elizabeth Daly (left) with Jesse Wolfe as Mutt.

Shaun Powell (left) with Jeremy Gold.

Jesse Wolfe (left) with Elizabeth Daly.

HANK: Hi, how are you?

MUTT (*for* MARGARET's *benefit*): Catholic, I'm told.

HANK (*naturally confused*): Ah. Well, I hope you'll soon be feeling better! I'm a lapsed Protestant, myself.

MARGARET: Is it really possible to *tell* if someone's a lapsed Protestant?

HANK: Well, I finally stopped *meaning* to get to church.

PRISS (*discreetly*): I guess we had better get going to this election party.

HANK: Right. Our caissons go rolling along.

PRISS: What are caissons, anyway?

HANK (*to* MUTT): Women. No grasp of ballistics.

MARGARET: No. We wage words.

HANK: And I surrender. It's nice to meet you at last. (*To* MUTT) And nice to meet you, Mutt.

MUTT: It's a dog meet dog world.

MARGARET: Good-bye! 'Bye Priss!

PRISS: Enjoy your evening. 'Bye Mutt!

HANK (*as handshakes are traded*): This is like a receiving line.

MUTT: Well, you're leaving, it's more like shipping than receiving. (HANK *laughs*)

HANK: Ha . . . ! Well, stop and visit next time you're up at R&B.

MUTT: Ooh, an egalitarian.

PRISS: Oh, Mutt! 'Bye, now. Don't get run over!

MUTT: 'Bye! (PRISS *and* HANK *go, leaving* MUTT *and* MARGARET *at a loss*) Who's that, her badminton partner?

MARGARET: She digs him, but it's unclear if he really digs her.

MUTT: Unrequited dig, too bad. Are you going to ask me to sit down?

MARGARET: It's probably not a good idea to leave your bike for too long, even if it's locked—

MUTT: I get it, the concerned brush-off. Thanks. How are you, though?

MARGARET (*surprisingly frank and upset*): Well, I don't have a job, I'm living here courtesy Priss, my mother's really sick but insists no one visit her, my brothers are all hiding their heads hoping it'll go away, and—I don't know if I'm jealous of Priss or scared for her. And, you're a sore for sore eyes.

MUTT (*an ill-advised joke*): You're unhappy. That's a turn-off. I liked you better angry.

MARGARET (*wincing*): I don't have the strength to try to figure you out. It's like looking for hay in a stack of needles. We seem to connect for a nanosecond at a time, like those man-made elements in the lab, and then it's back to lead. I can't take it. It's exhausting.

MUTT (*helplessly*): Well . . . I'll go, then.

MARGARET (*surprised by his thoughtfulness*): You will? That's very nice of you. (*Awkward, hopeful pause*)

MUTT: . . . So now I *have* to go! (*He puts on his helmet and goes, frustrated.* MARGARET *is doubly baffled. Blackout.*)

SCENE 18

PRISS' *and* MARGARET's *apartment.* PRISS *and* PONY *are heard off-stage, coming up the stairs.*
PRISS and PONY (*singing*): "Born is the king of Is-ra-el! (*They enter, in winter coats, with a few crumpled shopping bags*)

PONY: When I was little I thought it meant thanks to Jesus there would be no hell—(*Singing*)

No hell, no hell!

(*She takes their coats*) Oh, can I use your phone for a second? It's local.

PRISS: There it is. I'll make some cocoa, would you like that? Or would you like a drink?

PONY (*he wants a drink*): Boy, I sure would!

PRISS (*not hearing*): Oh, I forgot you're a Mormon! (*She goes to put on milk to boil*)

PONY (*dials phone, calls to* PRISS): Sitting in the front row at the movie was like falling through fireworks! Everything so huge and about to shoot right through you! (*Now, into phone, to a machine*) Hi! I just want you to know, I think you are wonderful. Keep a-goin', baby, keep a-goin'! I love you. 'Bye! (*He hangs up.* PRISS *has reappeared and is clearly intrigued.* PONY *explains*) I—I phoned my own answering machine. So I'll have encouragement when I get home.

PRISS (*sympathetically*): Oh, Pony! Haven't you made any commercial friends? Hank says you audition a lot.

PONY: Well, Hank's the best friend I've made, and it's real hard to see him.

PRISS: In many ways.

PONY: I hope it isn't sneaky of me to ask you out while he's away.

PRISS: No! Though I wish you'd let me pay for the movie.

PONY: Hey, I made a lot of money not understanding computers in that ad! (*He comically reenacts the baffled expression he had in the commercial*)

PRISS: Usually people pay my way for me to show they're aware my family has money.

PONY (*teasing outrage*): What? Beauty, brains, AND money!

PRISS: Yes, I've had a lot of advantages to overcome.

PONY (*meaning well*): Well, you sure have overcome them! (*Cautiously*) . . . I was wondering—Can I ask you something personal?

PRISS: If I said no, I'd go crazy wondering what you were wondering.

PONY: So, what is your status with Hank?

PRISS: I don't know. He has been very kind to me!

PONY: Do you think he's in love with you?

PRISS: Pony, I don't know. He's pretty independent.

PONY (*surprising himself with vehemence*): He's a wonderful guy!

PRISS (*mistaking this for guilty protest*): Pony, what's the matter? (MARGARET *enters, in coat, with her mail, very frustrated*)

MARGARET: AAaaargggh! (*She spies* PONY) Oh sorry! I hate to meet people while I'm screaming.

PRISS: Margaret, this is Pony Crocker, a friend of Hank's. Margaret Gaminski.

MARGARET: Hi! I was screaming because I got a rare envelope from home and I was trying to open it in the elevator and it fell between the gap there, down the shaft.

PONY: Can't you ask your super to get it?

MARGARET: No, I can't. Where have you two been, all pink?

PRISS: Pony took me to the movies and we did some shopping. (*Exits briefly*)

PONY: The Style Barn on 14th Street. Look—Misprinted
Mickey Mouse placemats. You get the nose here and the
ears there and in the middle, nothing! Three for a buck.
Plus, a swatch of fabric from Hitler's car! Probably phony!
Hank likes weird stuff.

MARGARET (*observant, but casual*): Ah, ha, presents for Hank?
So, do you know Hank from Houston? Are you a NASA
brat?

PONY: Oh, no! But I approve of outer space. I think it's going to
be very big. No, I'm an actor. Hank has sort of sponsored
me.

MARGARET: He *is* sponsorial. Acting, that takes endless persis-
tence!

PONY: I'm from a hard-working family. My sister, Juicy, once
wrote the letter *A* 18,000 times to get into the Guiness Book
of World Records! And then she didn't get in, there was no
such category. (PRISS *reenters with cocoa fixings on a tray*)

PRISS (*mock pride*): I've made the cocoa!

PONY: Can I offer another refreshment to cheer us up on this
cold night? (*He produces a vial of cocaine*)

PRISS (*disbelieving*): Cocaine, Good lord! Not for me! Did Dr.
Everything give you that?

PONY (*sensing her disapproval*): No, this guy from the Great
American Fizz keeps calling me, Greg. This was his Thanks-
giving gift.

MARGARET: (*reflexively declines*) No, but go ahead.

PRISS (*the concerned Mom*): Do you do a lot of that, Pony?

PONY (*self-conscious now, even scared*): N-no! I just got it!

MARGARET (*touched, to relieve him*): Oh Pony! I'll join you, if that'll help. He's even got a little spoon, how elfin. (*She and* PONY *snort*)

PRISS: When you and I are married, that will have to stop.

MARGARET: Whaaa-aat?

PRISS: Hank jokes that Pony and I would make wonderful parents.

MARGARET (*deadpan*): Oh, dear. I mean, How dear. (PONY *stands*)

PONY: Let's have some music! When I'm lonesome, I like the company of *vocals!*

PRISS: The records are in Margaret's room. It's the one with the autographed photo of the ape on the door. (PONY *goes off briefly*)

MARGARET (*turning on* PRISS) "Oh what a tangled web we weave When first we practice to reprieve!"

PRISS: Oh, stop. I'm just considering regrouping my affections. Here's someone with real needs.

MARGARET: Yes, a child's. Don't backslide into pity dates!

PRISS: He's been trying to find out how serious I am about Hank.

MARGARET: Oh, Priscilla! Wake up and smell the mocha mint! He's trying to find out how serious *Hank* is about *you!* People joke about marriage when it's out of the question. Ohh, this stuff is making me dizzy. (PRISS *takes in* MARGARET's *logical appraisal. Ill-chosen but boisterous music comes from offstage, and* PONY *reappears, wiggling suggestively under the cocaine's impetus*)

PONY (*dancing*): Anybody want to dance?

(*Blackout.*)

END ACT ONE.

ACT TWO

ACT TWO

ACT II

SCENE 1

MUTT's *hangout, the NYU frat. On the same ratty couch on which he'd watched porno, he and* HANK *are having some late-night beers. On* MUTT's *can is a gag device peddled through magazine ads called a "beer boob," which is a breast-shaped attachment through which one drinks. The two men have become friends. It's the last day of February, Leap Year Day. Both sing, badly, a tune very like but not enough like "All Of Me" to require royalty payments.*

BOTH: . . . I give the section
  That is my erection,
  But never quite all of meee! . . . (*They laugh*)

MUTT: . . . Hey, you're not using your beer boob!

HANK (*grossed out*): Oh, come on!

MUTT (*he grins, a bit sozzled*): I'm enjoying getting you drunk, it's like pulling the head off a Ken doll!

HANK: You think I'm false and I'm not, I'm jus' healthy! New Yorkers are suspicious of health, they think only neurosis is honest.

MUTT: I'm not a New Yorker, pal, but I do think with all the money you make, you could at least have the decency to be discontent.

HANK: So what's with you? You can't be as dumb as I think you are. You could apply yourself.

MUTT: Well, I do in a way, but my greatness will be lost to history.

HANK: Oh, and what's that?

MUTT (*mock bashfully*): I can come seven times in one night.

HANK (*playing along*): Seven times! Doesn't life start seeming inane around number four?

MUTT: It's the principle of the thing.

HANK: Well, your greatness might not remain unknown. One of your partners might tell. (*Pause*)

MUTT: . . . Partners?

HANK: The women you were with.

MUTT: . . . With? (*Pause*) Oh! Right. No, that kind of thing puts me off these days. I hate feeling judged.

HANK: But don't you like feeling witnessed?

MUTT: Well, I'm gettin' on in years. I don't want to be concentrated on. I'm slowin' down. I've got nostril hair, there's yellow saliva in my mouth when I wake up, and my shit smells like my Dad's used to, *that's* scary. I'm so out of it. I don't have any credit cards, I don't floss, I don't cook, I don't have an IRA, I don't *share*, I'm just like my old man—I'm for real, I'm not modern.

HANK: Wow. You know, everyone fascinates me, but your intentional failure is particularly interesting. (*He gets up to replace his beer*)

MUTT: Hey, there used to be lots of women in my life! I used to follow my dick around like a dowsing rod. It was easy then. If only I knew now what I knew then. . . .

HANK: Personally, I wouldn't be eighteen again if you put a gun to my head.

MUTT: You sure wouldn't. In fact, it would probably age you a little.

HANK (*proffering another beer to* MUTT): Well, here's to Leap Year Day! Thanks for letting me hide out here! (*Drinks*)

MUTT: Afraid Priss might propose? What's going on with you and her?

HANK: Well, I do want a co-anchor, but I don't know. We spent New Year's Eve together. That's the iron maiden of dates, trapped in the gesture of you and her facing the future together. Then she gave me walkie–talkies for Valentine's Day. To improve our communication, I guess. I don't know. I'm moved by her anxiousness, and sometimes it's hilarious. She locks the bathroom door if she's gonna blow her nose. She's so scared, it's adorable!

MUTT: So—are you gonna move in together?

HANK: Well, I think so. I feel I owe her at least that, to show her I did give it a try. (*Beat*) What about you and Margaret? You don't see each other—does that mean it's serious?

MUTT: She's too messed up, and she makes me feel messed up, which I don't want to feel even if it's true. What's the old line? (*He replaces the 'beer boob' on* HANK's *can*) "Never eat at a place called Mom's" . . . somethin' somethin' . . .

"And never sleep with anyone whose problems are worse than yours."

HANK (*improvising drunkenly*): And never sleep with anyone called Mom.

MUTT (*he doesn't like this joke*): Yike! (*He sips from his 'beer boob'*)

HANK (*shrugging*): I never knew my Mom. She died when I was born. I was 13 pounds. Too healthy. (*Pause*)

MUTT: Are you all right?

HANK (*shakes off his grave pause*): Yeah . . . I've had a wide selection of stepmothers, though . . . ! (*He makes to drink, but confronts the 'beer boob' MUTT has affixed to the can*) These things are ridiculous.

(*Blackout.*)

SCENE 2

PONY *is visiting* MARGARET; PRISS *is out. He wears a tropical shirt with the sleeves rolled too far up. She wears an enormous wooden rosary, its beads the size of lemons, a Caribbean tourist novelty. She is looking at photos from* PONY'*s location shooting.*
MARGARET: Mmmm, I can see how that jungle could pass for Venus.

PONY: No apes. I asked.

MARGARET: There are no apes in the New World.

PONY: Here I am on the set. Supposedly I've just taken off. They add the sky around you later. It's called blue screen.

MARGARET: And is this some voodoo priestess?

PONY: That's the woman at the market who makes the rosaries.

MARGARET (*shaking her beads like chains*): Well, as long as it's to make money, and she doesn't actually believe in it.

PONY: When I told her my name was Anthony, she told me he's the patron saint of lost objects.

MARGARET: Oh, right! I always liked that, the guys on Christ's cabinet. (*She removes the clattering huge rosary*) I can't wear this for long, I'd get stooped!

PONY: It's just a joke gift for you. April Fool's and Easter at once. "I'm saving mankind! No, just kidding!"

MARGARET: It was sweet of you to weigh down your luggage for me.

PONY: Well, I'm grateful for our little sessions. I like stopping by.

MARGARET: Well, without my chimp to rear, I'm at loose ends, too.

PONY: Priss has been treating me strangely, though, when I see her.

MARGARET (*tactfully*): Er . . . She's under some strain. Her twin brother is getting married—to an Olympic skier.

PONY: Is that bad?

MARGARET: No, but she sees it symbolically, and she doesn't know what it symbolizes.

PONY: Well, she's really very lucky.

MARGARET (*the cagey therapist*): Did you get Hank anything?

PONY: A couple of things, little things. (*But he doesn't elaborate*) You know, they're so happy together, and you and I get along so well . . .

MARGARET (*deflectively*): Pebbles and Bam Bam. (PONY *takes her hand as if to play a love scene*) What?

PONY: Thanks for putting up with me! (*He hugs her reflexively, fumblingly*)

MARGARET: Pony! (*He tries to kiss her, as if directed to. She breaks loose uncomfortably*) Pony, this isn't high school. There's no required prom date! (*He looks downcast*) Oh, no!

PONY: You don't want me. (MARGARET *is boggled, like a baby-sitter set upon by a toddler*)

MARGARET (*significantly*): Pony, sit down. There's something I have to tell you. (*He sits*) It's something I've known for some time, and I just feel you should know, too. I hope this won't affect our friendship. (*Pause*) Pony . . . You're gay. (*He seems dazed by this news*) I think you knew that, didn't you?

PONY (*finally*): I guess I did. When I first got here a hooker in Times Square asked me to go out and I said, "No, Thanks," and she said, "Oh, a Gay Boy!" And I said to myself, "Boy, they sure see through you fast in this city!" (*Pause*) So I made a deal with God. If he'd overlook it, I would. And I had some good luck, so I promised I'd be, you know, celibate.

MARGARET: Another secret scandal of show biz.

PONY: But I was all alone. So we added a clause that said I could drink and do drugs.

MARGARET: Oh, Pony. I didn't think people still fell down that hole. Does your family know, do you think?

PONY: I don't know. My mother's real squeamish about these things. She has yet to acknowledge heterosexuality.

MARGARET: Well, as long as *you* know what *you're* going through. You realize, though, that Hank is not going to give you what you think you need. . . .

PONY (*reluctantly*): I guess.

MARGARET: Well, nothing seemed to be happening, did it?

PONY: I couldn't tell.

MARGARET: If you can't tell, then nothing is. I think you're just stubborn, you imprinted on him, like a chick mistaking a Stop sign for its father—(*The phone rings*) Excuse me.

PONY (*this is a lot to handle*): Is there anything to drink?

MARGARET: I don't know, go ahead and look. (*He does; she answers the phone*) Hello? (*Her face instantly drains*)

PONY (*offstage*): Hey! Champagne!

MARGARET: JoAnn, what's wrong . . . ? Is it Mom . . . ?
Then, what . . . ? Oh, no . . . Oh, no . . . Oh, no . . .
(*Ghastly silence as she listens.* PONY *reappears, sensing something is wrong. He holds a bottle of champagne from the
refrigerator. He stands by, ready but awkward*) I'll come
right home. . . . It's just . . . How is she . . . ? Yeah
. . . I will . . . Oh, JoAnn . . . I'll call you back when I
know the flight. . . . I love you. (*Hangs up with a weird
expression on her face, like a victim of a perplexing joke*) My
Dad died. (*He goes to hold her, and she relents helplessly,
clutching him. He doesn't know how to put down the champagne bottle, though, and it waves behind her back. Blackout.*)

SCENE 3

MUTT *and* MARGARET *sit on a bench in Greenwich Village, survey-
ing the passing parade. Late May, early evening.* MUTT *wears
trendy black clothes, like a SoHo clubgoer.*
MUTT (*commenting on passersby unseen by us*): Yike, look at
her . . . ! Okay, boys, the sun's gone down, let's remove
the sunglasses! Innocent youth hoping to be mistaken for
drug addicts. (*Carefully*) So—How have you been?

MARGARET: Well, it's been intense. I always thought I never
thought about my Dad. He was at the firehouse or asleep
most of the time. But the closure somehow is bringing back
a lot of things I'd forgotten. . . . He used to honk the horn
for us when we drove through tunnels . . . cut my keilbasy
up for me . . . stand at the back window watching the
grackles in the snow. . . . He and my mom won the egg
toss at the parish picnic. You have to toss a raw egg back and

forth without breaking it. That's a sign of a good marriage, isn't it? (*Pause*) She was amazingly together. She kept telling all of us not to worry about her, that she was ready, too. . . . "We lived to see you grow up, that's all we wanted. . . ." And what humbles me, who wants everything, is . . . she's telling the truth. (*She dwells inwardly on her Mother's newly glimpsed profundity*)

MUTT: . . . My old man died hauling a refrigerator out of a deadbeat's house. He owed somebody a favor. No friends, but he did a lot of favors. (*Pause*) They used to pay him off in singles. Like, to put him down, even when they owed him something. . . . What could he do, he took it. . . . (*He finds himself unexpectedly bitter*) It's not evil that gets caught and punished. . . . It's clumsiness . . . (*Pause. Now MARGARET must comfort him*)

MARGARET: Ohh . . . Say. You look almost Cro Magnon in those new clothes.

MUTT (*brightens*): Thanks. I take compliments really well.

MARGARET: When did you desert the messenger service for the club scene?

MUTT: Ehh, the owners decided to upgrade their image, you know, gentrify it. The idea was cyclists in Brooks Brothers suits, strictly white, no homeboys, no hoods—They changed the name to Preppin' Fetchit—and they fired everyone but me.

MARGARET: That must have hurt your pride.

MUTT: So I quit.

MARGARET: Poor Tarzan. But another vine came along?

MUTT: I'm working at Fata Morgana full-time now, as the bouncer. They all admire how real I am.

MARGARET: And how real are they?

MUTT: Well, they must exist. Morgana provides the wardrobe. She says she's *furnishing a dream*. Her picture's in the papers a lot, she's sort of secretly famous.

MARGARET: Morgana? Is that her real name?

MUTT: It is, but she herself is made up.

MARGARET: . . . And, are you seeing anyone?

MUTT (*unsurely, after a pause*): Do you want me to answer that honestly?

MARGARET (*she knows what that must mean*): I think you just did.

MUTT: Well, seeing, if not believing. It's strictly physical. I hear drums, but no violins.

MARGARET (*intuitively*): This Morgan entity. (MUTT *shrugs helplessly*)

MUTT: I've never been in a scene before.

MARGARET: All this hanging out with the artsy set—Are you still a bigot?

MUTT: I don't know. I hope not.

MARGARET: Well, better confusion than prejudice! (PONY *appears, in sunglasses. He wears a conservative suit*)

PONY: Margaret?

MARGARET: Pony? (*They embrace emotionally, to* MUTT'*s concerned surprise*)

PONY: Welcome back! How are you! I missed you! (MARGARET *realizes how this might look, but decides to enjoy it*)

MARGARET: Pony, this is Mutt Vespucci. Mutt, Pony Crocker.

PONY and MUTT (*simultaneously*): Nice suit!

MARGARET: What are you doing down here?

PONY: I'm looking at an apartment!

MARGARET: To buy?

PONY (*making a face*): Yes, to buy! (*Points to himself*) "Look out, it's an adult!"—It's a 'prewar classic' over on Greenwich, by the Church of the Exquisite Panic. I'm wearing the suit to make a good impression on their board.

MUTT (*grinning*): Just be careful, they might think you were a canvasing Mormon! (*This makes for an awkward moment*)

PONY: . . . Well, I'd, uh, better get going. I'm due there five minutes ago! I will call you. Nice to meet you! (*He removes his sunglasses*) It's getting too dark for these, isn't it? I will, I'll call!

MARGARET: 'Bye! (PONY *goes.* MARGARET *smiles smugly. Is* MUTT *jealous?*)

MUTT: You've got someone else. That's hot.

(*Blackout.*)

SCENE 4

HANK's *office. He and* PRISS, *again apparently idle, discuss a project of* HANK's. *It's late June.*
HANK: They want to call it KNOX KNOCKS. (*He demonstrates with gestures, pointing to himself and then knocking*) KNOX KNOCKS. What do you think?

PRISS: I don't know. I had a teacher at Milton who said, "Superior minds discuss ideas, and inferior minds discuss people."

HANK: What a stupid old woman!

PRISS: How do you know it was a woman?

HANK: Well, wasn't it?

PRISS (*sheepishly, bested*): Yes.

HANK: The point is, people are ideas. Essences in sausage casings. Numbers made numerals. I can show that!

PRISS: But it sounds like some lurid peek-a-boo, famous people revealing their personal problems on television—*especially* while conducting tours of their homes—

HANK: It could do a lot of good, like global therapy. They tune in for glitz and get support on Sexual Abuse, Obesity, Mastectomy, Vasectomy, Religion—All that. (*Beat*) Plus, the swimming pools shaped like their faces. Call it . . . psychotainment.

PRISS (*doubtfully*): Is there such a thing as ostentatious humiliation?

HANK (*fondly, a smidge condescendingly*): My little Puritan!

PRISS (*after a pause*): Hank . . . I think we should stop seeing each other.

HANK (*grinning*): Now . . . Does that mean you think we should get married? (*But it's no joke, and his grin fades*) I'm sorry. I'm sorry. I'm sorry. Is that enough?

PRISS (*childish pride*): No.

HANK (*adding one more to the pile*): I'm sorry.

PRISS (*placated*): That's enough.

HANK (*trying to reassure her*): Hey, let's get away somewhere. How about Miniature America, out there in Pennsylvania Dutch Country? World's biggest miniature, the whole country on a tabletop. Factories, towns, circus grounds, the Rockies, even an Indian Reservation. They light it up at night, it's hilarious. And, there's a motel for us gigantic humans. . . .

PRISS: Didn't you hear what I said? Doesn't what I say count?

HANK: Yes, but do you really mean it? Do you break all your dishes to keep them from breaking later? Look, does your

father's offer to use your Cape Cod place still hold? Let's go
up there next weekend, get some negative ions, try out our
walkie–talkies in the open spaces. Touch base with beauty.
(PRISS *hesitates. It is appealing*) We can take Margaret, too.
(*Points to himself*) Thoughtful person?

PRISS: I never said you weren't thoughtful. You're recklessly
thoughtful! Like we're all your charity cases. (PONY *appears,
with his now professional leather photo–and–resumé case*)

PONY: Hi! There's nobody at the reception desk, so I just loped
on back. . . . (*Senses a slight awkwardness*) Is this an okay
time?

PRISS: Historians are still debating that.

PONY: I mean, to stop by for a second. I was in the building. . . .

HANK: Sure, Pony! We've got some sugar cubes for ya here
somewhars! We were just planning a little Cape Cod weekend.

PONY: You were?

HANK (*plunging on, but realizing this fatal social impasse*): . . .
Yes. Tell Priss she's *got* to go!

PONY: Priss, it sounds great! I've never been.

HANK (*trapped by his social grace*): Er . . . would you like to
join us? (PRISS *hates this suggestion*) We'd need a partner for
Margaret, anyway.

PRISS (*lightly, but* HANK *gets the message*): You're too thoughtful!

HANK (*helplessly pressing on*): Do you sail?

PONY: I don't know if I do. I haven't yet. I'd love to, thanks! (*Envisioning the fun*) We can sing chanteys! How's your writing going, Priss?

PRISS: Oh, nothing much. Just my resumé and my suicide note.

HANK (*to keep it light*): Priss believes in options.

PRISS (*sparing* PONY *any anxiety*): Don't worry, Pony, both of them are works of fiction! How's your acting scene?

PONY: I'm up for the lead in a sci–fi movie!

HANK (*still sweating*): Aren't we all?

PRISS (*she stands to go*): I have some work to do, incredible as that sounds. I'll see you next weekend, then, Pony! Good luck with the sci–fi! Hank, you are too good!

HANK: I know, I'm sorry.

PRISS: Yes, we can finish that tally later. (*She goes.* PONY *seems agitated*)

HANK: So, is something the matter?

PONY: No! But it is a final call-back. They saw me in the robot commercial. Today I'm supposed to scream when my brain is removed.

HANK: Lord a'mighty! (*Pause*)

PONY (*awfully*): Um . . . I can't go on like this with you.

HANK (*manfully trying to deal with this*): I know. Pony, not all love is sexual. Even sex isn't always sexual. Wait, back up. I mean, not having sex always seems like sex, but sex itself is about how sex isn't the answer. (*He's muddled and so is* PONY)

PONY: I think you're being too vague.

HANK: I don't want a sexual relationship with you, Pony.

PONY: I think you're being too frank.

HANK: I'm not your father, I'm not your brother, I'm not a thumb to suck. I can't fulfill you. People fulfill themselves. I will hug you. No kisses. Well, maybe, on the cheek, once you're famous. Long handshakes, no problem.

PONY: I see. That's all I'd ask for.

HANK: You say you see, but I don't see you seeing.

PONY: Well, can I touch you sometimes, just hold you? And think great thoughts?

HANK: In my experience, touching and thinking don't mix. Besides, once you start negotiating things like this, you can never have peace. Now, after they remove your brain, make sure you dig out this infatuation, because we can have a great friendship. Hello? (PONY *is silent*) Are you still up for this weekend? You don't have to be.

PONY (*marshalling his strength unconvincingly*): No, I want to . . . to show I can deal with it.

HANK: Are you sure your little Pony engine can handle that?

PONY (*serious and earnest*): I think I can . . . ! (*Pause*) . . . I
think I can . . .

(*Blackout.*)

SCENE 5

*Fata Morgana, a week and a half later. Loud music makes the
scene that follows a shouting match. Colored light. It's late at
night, and* PONY, *a beer in each hand, stands depressed.* MUTT
*comes by with a cardboard case of empties. They see each
other.*

PONY and MUTT (*simultaneously*): Hey . . . ! Margaret's friend!

PONY: Pony!

MUTT: Mutt! (*Awkwardly*) So! Loitering with intent to boogie?

PONY: Nope! Just standing still!

MUTT: Yeah, that's the courting dance in here!

PONY (*wondering if* MUTT *is gay*): It is so hard to meet anyone!

MUTT: No one *ever* meets anyone! (*Beat*)

PONY: That can't be true, can it?

MUTT: I mean in here!

PONY: Oh! Right! Water, Water Everywhere! (*Awkward pause*)

BOTH (*simultaneously, shouting*): You realize this is Gay Night?

PONY: Oh! Yes! Don't worry, I know!

MUTT (*figures he'd better nip this in the bud*): I'm not! I just work here! I'm a mercenary! I don't have to approve of the people I work for! I'd *starve* if I waited that long! (*Beat*) So does Margaret know about you?

PONY: It was Margaret who told me! (*This puzzles* MUTT, *but also relieves him*)

MUTT: Yeah? Well, brrr!! It must be a scary life! All those guys with the bodies of Nazis and the faces of victims!

PONY: It is! But I figure the odds are a little bit better here than in my apartment! And if I keep playing the machine, sooner or later all the cherries will line up! Jackpot!

MUTT: But . . . Aren't you scared? About—?

PONY (*this is odd, since both men have to shout over the music*): AIDS?
    . . . Yes!
But I took the test! It was negative! I haven't been exposed! My health is good! (*Pause*) Now I have no good explanation for my depression! (*He downs the remains of a beer*)

MUTT: Hey! Easy on the two–for–one!

PONY (*not dealing with that*): I'm seeing Margaret this weekend!

MUTT: You are?

PONY: We're going to her friend Priscilla's summer house!

MUTT: Oh sure! I worked on that place! (*Beat*) Do you have some kind of tortured thing with Margaret?

PONY: No, no! So you're welcome to!

MUTT: Hah! Well, it's all a mystery! (*Pause*) Ehh, we're all Sunday drivers. I better get back to the door! (*Pause*) Hey, just for my education . . . What is it that makes a man want another man?

PONY: I don't know. . . . If a man approves of me, it makes me feel straight.

MUTT: . . . Well, good luck! Maybe I'll see you this weekend. (*Exits.* PONY *resumes gazing outward and, despite the loud music, begins to sing to himself, jamming on the melody*)

PONY: Swing low, sweet chariot . . .
Comin' for to carry me home . . . !

(*Blackout.*)

SCENE 6

PONY, HANK, MARGARET *and* PRISS *are driving up to the Cape. The ride is almost over, and everyone's patience is wearing thin. The car is probably suggested by two benches, with the rear one sufficiently elevated to present* PONY *and* MARGARET *in the back seat.* HANK *is driving. The scene can also be prerecorded and heard on tape in darkness, to save staging headaches and to suggest "transition"—with* MUTT *coming onstage alone at scene's end to wave at the offstage arriving characters.*
PONY (*in conclusion, singing*)
All things shall perish from under the sky!

Music alone shall live (—Aw, come on!—)
Music alone shall live
Music alone shall live,
Never to die! (*No one's participated*)
It isn't much of a round if I'm the only one singing.

HANK: Sorry, Pony. I guess I think rounds are square.

PONY: Let's just try that refrain.

MARGARET: Why don't you just try *to* refrain?

PRISS (*playing the mother, up front*): Children!

PONY: Priss is in the Mom Seat.

PRISS: It's also the death seat, statistically.

HANK: Don't, that makes me very nervous!

MARGARET: "Fairburn Heiress Killed in Crash With Future Famous Friends."

HANK: Stop it!

MARGARET (*craning to look back as they pass*): Look at that sign! Flee Market—F–L–E–E!

PONY: Is that wrong? They probably *are* moving.

PRISS (*barely containing her frustration with* PONY): Eek.

HANK (*determined*): Now come on, campers, we're almost there!

PONY (*helping to keep things chipper*): I love your car, Hank!

HANK (*good-natured tease to* PRISS): It's not mine, I rented it! I'm not ready to commit to one vehicle. I'd have to park it. (*Grins at* PRISS; *she makes a face or groans*)

PRISS (*uneasily*): Now just follow this toward the ocean. (*Beat. As confidentially as she can, she speaks to* HANK *alone*) Isn't something very wrong here?

HANK (*determined*): Not officially. I don't recognize its right to be.

PRISS (*to the back seat*): Almost there!

PONY (*singing*): Almost there, almost there!

HANK (*grim Daddy*): Pony, please!

PONY: Sorry. (*Pause. He tries to buck up*) I wish we could get along like your chimpanzees, Margaret, grooming each other and grinning all the time. Playing pat-a-cake . . .

MARGARET: Don't look to apes for inspiration, they make war and eat meat and shun their cripples just like us. And that grin is to show they're scared.

PONY: How disillusioning.

PRISS: Here, here! Turn up here! (*They now bump up a dirt drive*)

PONY: Will any of your immediate family be here?

PRISS: No, it's just us. (*Pause*) My family's not the immediate
  kind. They're more the call-ahead-first type.

(HANK *negotiates the dirt drive to the house*)

PONY: But somebody's there. On the porch!

PRISS: Or something! It's soaking wet! Bigfoot?

MARGARET (*furious? Or impressed?*): It's Mutt!

(*Blackout.*)

SCENE 7

The deck of the beach house, that night. PRISS *and* MARGARET *sit
on the deck chairs; the deck railing is a clue to the setting; a
tiny bug candle, remains of food, some liquor bottles, two other
chairs.* PRISS *wears a black swimsuit.* MARGARET *is still fully
dressed. Both nurse drinks. Faint surf sounds, maybe shouts
from the offstage men.*

MARGARET: Why are you wearing your black swimsuit?

PRISS: I am in mourning for my beach party.

MARGARET: Oh, no, Mother Discourage! Your problem is that
  whenever anything good happens you say "Well, this *moment* is good," but whenever anything bad happens you say
  "*Life* is awful!"

PRISS: When did you get so upbeat?

MARGARET: I'm compromising myself for your sake. Checks and
  balances.

PRISS: I think you're flattered that Mutt showed up.

MARGARET: Well, my job starts soon, that helps. (*Beat*) Brrr— Aren't you cold? (*She puts a towel around* PRISS' *shoulders*)

PRISS (*shrugging*): No. Pony's still running around in his Speedos.

PONY (*way off, distant and drunk*): Look! Dead Man's Float!

PRISS: Poor thing. He lives an octave higher than written.

MARGARET: And he's full of more dangerous chemicals tonight than the River Ganges.

PONY (*again, distant*): No, I can do it this time!

PRISS: You have to admit, Mutt's coming uninvited and unwelcome was pretty heroic.

MARGARET: Are you encouraging me now?

PRISS: Look at the beautiful work he did on this place.

MARGARET (*of two minds*): But isn't he a jerk? Aren't they all?

PRISS: Well? Is he *your kind* of jerk? Checks and balances.

(*The men return, in swimsuits,* PONY *wettest of all*)

PONY (*as they appear, singing*):
Who did, who did, who did, who did,
Who did swallow Jo, Jo, Jo, Jo,
Who did swallow Jonah down?

MUTT: The Phantom of the Square Dance.

PRISS: Having fun, Pony?

PONY: I'm getting there!

HANK: I think you rode past your stop.

PONY (*sings*):
   Ezekiel saw the wheel way up in the middle of the air . . . !
   (*Spoken*)
   They say the wheel Ezekiel saw was the first UFO.

HANK (*deadpan*): I'm calling the police.

PONY (*extravagantly*): I'm sor'! I'm kidding, I don't believe in it,
   I don't! I'm jus' kidding! Anyway, it's Baptist! I jus' like how
   it sounds! All achey and beautiful!

MUTT: Sure. Jesus becomes you.

PONY: So, you believe in Jesus?

MUTT: Well . . . I have Elvis' Christmas album.

PONY (*meddling with the liquor bottles*): Let's have a nightcap
   together! (*Pleading, but appealingly*) We have to toast together once! To show we know it's not poisoned!

PRISS: Why not? I'd like to erase this day from my mental
   Etch–A–Sketch.

(PONY *pours Collins mix on top of the vodka shots*)

HANK: Careful, Pony! You're not a movie star yet!

(*They drink, and* PONY *sighs sentimentally.* PRISS *acts to avoid bathos*)

PRISS: Shall we play word games or something? That's what my folks always do here! They end up running to the OED to challenge each other's usage.

MARGARET: How alien. With my folks it was a boilermaker and Polka Varieties.

MUTT: My mother isn't allowed to enjoy herself.

MARGARET: That's awful!

MUTT: Hey, she's the boss, she made the rule.

HANK: My Dad and stepmother don't have any friends, so they have people over all the time.

PONY (*abruptly*): Hey! (*This gets him their attention*) Speaking of parents, you know something I noticed? You know in paintings? (*He seems to expect an answer, but after a moment, continues*) You see *Mary* at the crucifixion, but where's *Joseph?* Come on, where is he? (*He gets worked up over this trivia, as the drunk do*) There's Mary carrying on, but where is Joseph? Couldn't she get him to come? Didn't he care? "Come on, your son only gets crucified once!" "Oh, you go, Mary, I'm tired!" (*This might be funnier if* PONY *weren't so impassioned*)

PRISS: Please, no more about Christ, it's unwholesome!

(PONY *starts to cry*)

PRISS: Oh no.

HANK: Pony . . . (PONY *breaks away*)

MUTT (*trying to lighten things up*): Absolut corrupts absolutely!

(*All of them except* MUTT *instinctively lean toward* PONY, *but to* HANK's *credit,* HANK *cradles him*)

HANK: Pony, Pony, it's all right. . . .

PONY (*mystified by his own sobs*): I don't care about Jesus, I don't! I don't know what it is! It isn't about anything!

MARGARET: He's so tired. . . . (PONY *subsides, and is still confused by his own outburst*)

PONY: I'm sorry! I had a really wonderful day! I don't understand this!

MUTT: Too much nature.

MARGARET (*helping* HANK): Pony, it's very natural. Alcohol, dead of night, the ocean—They open gulfs in us—.

HANK: Here, I'll take him in. Come on, Pony, yeah . . . Things will look even worse in the morning. But you will be fine the day after.

PONY (*as if leaving for a long voyage*): Good night! Good night! It's all right! I'm not your enemy, Priss, I'm not!

PRISS (*surprised, but does her best*): Of course not, Pony!

(HANK *carries* PONY *off, who is arguably Christlike in his Speedos and faintness. A pall hangs*)

MUTT: Well, that joyride ended up in the gully.

PRISS (*the shattered hostess*): This is turning into a weekend of terror.

MARGARET: He must feel alone here. You'd think getting that movie role would reassure him.

PRISS: And it will, I'm sure. He's still learning how to drink too much.

MUTT: Well, I crashed the party but at least I didn't collapse.

MARGARET: Is that going to be your epitaph?

MUTT: Good thing I know those darts are rubber. (HANK *returns*)

HANK: I lay him down and he went to sleep, or passed out, if there's a difference.

MARGARET (*everyone's pretty helpless*): He'll be all right. He's going through a rough time in his life. Out of the womb.

HANK (*standing behind* PRISS' *chair*): Shall we go in, too . . . ? Mmm. I love you.

PRISS (*startled*): Why do you say that?

HANK (*reassuringly*): Because I like you. (*He says his goodnights*) Good night all.

PRISS: Good night. (HANK *leads her in*)

MARGARET: Good night, Hank, good night, Priss!

(*Pause.* MUTT *and* MARGARET *are alone*)

MUTT: So . . . ! Potentially nice night.

MARGARET (*warily*): Hmh . . .

MUTT: God sure sneezed a lot of stars!

MARGARET: I do like how the Milky Way Galaxy looks as if it were going down the drain. . . . And how are you doing?

MUTT: Just processing my dinner, working up a big bowel movement. (*Pause*)

MARGARET (*dryly*): You're a busy man.

MUTT (*smiling*): I really will be. I got a new job.

MARGARET: You quit Morgana? What will she think?

MUTT: Think is not an operative verb with her. Pony bought a coop and I'm doing the makeover.

MARGARET: That's great! And I have a new job, too! I mean, my old job at last! Lorn Burks, the man who made the charges, he had to be institutionalized, and Spiegel's urban nurture project is on again! And I'm his aide-de-chimp!

MUTT: Teaching Bobo to use a crosswalk and wait in line?

MARGARET: And eventually, to jaywalk and push in front of people!

MUTT: Congratulations! (*They hug—a first—and it goes from impetuous to mellow*) Mmm. (*Pause. They take in the night*) The moon up there, like a luminous fingernail clipping.

MARGARET (*visualizing this*): Urk. *Luminous.* You know the ex-cons I was tutoring in reading and writing?

MUTT: I don't think so, but you never know.

MARGARET: I gave one of them some vocabulary words to make sentences with, and one of the words was *luminous.* And this guy wrote, "When you come out of solitary confinement, everything is *luminous.*" (*Pause. They kiss*) Wo.

MUTT: Do you mean Whoa like Stop? Or Woe like grief?

MARGARET: Wo like . . . unfinished Wow.

(*They kiss again. Blackout.*)

SCENE 8

The same, the deck, the next morning, very early. PRISS *is wrapped in a blanket and sits in a deck chair, fitfully trying to write in a notebook, but unable to.* MARGARET *appears, her ebullience opposed to* PRISS' *bleakness.*

MARGARET: Hey . . . ! Trouble sleeping?

PRISS: No. Trouble wide awake.

MARGARET: Aww. (*Smiling and stretching*) I slept the sleep of the guilty—deep and thoughtless.

PRISS: I've been up all night. When I couldn't sleep I got dressed and came out here. I thought if I sat in a cold chair fully dressed, I'd fall asleep just to be contrary. But my body seems to need reverse reverse psychology.

MARGARET: What are you writing?

PRISS: What else? Nothing. I look out at the ocean, I feel like I should be getting great ideas, but I'm not.

MARGARET: But isn't that the point of nature? To help free you from ideas? (*Takes* PRISS' *notebook and reads from it*) "I need psychiatric help." Oh, Priss.

PRISS: I took a walk on the beach, about an hour ago, in that gray before day, and I felt cold, but like you say, the waves coming in seemed to say, stop fighting, accept, get over this idea of ideas. And just when I said, "Okay, I Accept," this couple rode by on a horse, through the surf.

MARGARET: A horse? Around here?

PRISS: Unsaddled. I swear, a man and a woman. I didn't see their faces. And the way she held him and he held the horse, I don't know, it was preposterous, it promised beauty and togetherness *I know cannot be.*

MARGARET: Could you have imagined it?

PRISS: What difference does it make?

MARGARET: You'll be fine, you just need sleep.

(PRISS *finally notices how charged* MARGARET *is*)

PRISS: You're so galvanized today. (*She suddenly gets the idea*) Margaret! B.C.?

MARGARET: A.D.!

PRISS: How earth-shattering!

MARGARET (*a ruminated correction*): Mmm, earth-cohering.

PRISS: Eek! How do you feel?

MARGARET (*shrugs*): Happy. Sad. Is there a word for both at once?

PRISS (*indulgently*): How about Sappy?

MARGARET: It's true. I'm innocent now. Sex has shattered my worldliness.

(PONY *enters, still in swimsuit, gingerly*)

PONY: Oooooooohhhhh . . .

MARGARET: Good morning. Risen from the dead!

PONY (*sweet-tempered despite his hangover*): I never quite died. Oooh, my headache's where my halo should be. Or my devil horns.

MARGARET: Or your antennae.

PONY: There was some strange noise all night, like raccoons under the house. Oh, well. Uhh! I'll bet I had fun last night. Did I do anything? I'm sorry if I did!

PRISS: No, nothing, Pony!

MARGARET (MARGARET *hugs* PONY, *sharing her new hope*): Pony, you have so much love to give, and when you are a movie star, people eager to love you will line up and all you'll have to do is choose the least insincere! How about that Greg guy from the Fizz ad?

PONY (*heartened*): You think . . . ? All I want is to be a part of it all.

MARGARET: As if you could help it! (*Looks out to the water*) I love morning. The day hasn't been tracked up yet.

PRISS (*recalling her duties*): Shall I put on some coffee?

PONY (*hangover, remember*): Oh, no thanks! But a swim might help clear my head.

MARGARET: A swim *will* help. Salt water is the same saline solution as the bloodstream.

PONY (*rather dashing, all considered*): Well! I guess My Ocean and The Ocean better get together! Thanks for including me. Happy Sunday!

(*He runs off, to hit the waves full speed. The women watch him for a long moment.* HANK *enters, casually dressed, breathes deeply the sea air, and places his fingertips to his temples like a psychic*)

HANK: Mmmmmm. I'm receiving a message. . . . "Dear Hank . . . Hope you're well . . . I know I am. Love, Nature."

MARGARET: Nature writes such nice letters.

PRISS (*remembering the horse in the surf*): Sometimes she over-writes.

HANK (*thickly Texan*): N' how' r' yew two nymphs this mawnin', nymph nymph?

MARGARET (*unprecedentedly friendly*): Purty saucy ma'self. (*She puts her hands on* HANK'*s shoulders, as if to dance*)

HANK (*amazed*): Margaret, do you mock?

MARGARET (*going back inside*): No, I play along!

HANK (*stares after her a moment*): . . . She's pixilated!

PRISS: She had a near-life experience last night.

HANK: You mean . . . ? (*Now he gets it*) Well, cut m'legs off 'n' call me Shorty! Love is in the air! (PRISS *is recovering, but is still strangely subdued*)

PRISS: Pony even seems revived. (HANK *sees him in the distance*)

HANK: Oh yes! I think he's over me. (*He sits and takes* PRISS' *hand*) There's no present like the present. (*They enjoy that present for a moment*)

PRISS (*finally*): Hank, we need to talk.

HANK: I know. But . . . can I just say something before we talk?

PRISS: Of course.

HANK: You know, I've missed you. Not just when I was out of
town, but when I was with you. You're so committed to un-
happiness.

PRISS: I know . . .

HANK: And I admit, I'm—growing up all over—different stepmothers—Thailand, Mexico, Illinois, Texas—all beautiful
places—but they were never quite real, I could never get
too involved. I knew enough not to need too much. And I
know I've resisted a certain kind of . . . surrender.

PRISS: Is it a war?

HANK (*irked at her turnabout*): You're the one who—(*But he
quickly checks his complaint and rearranges his tender clasp*)
You're high-strung, but maybe I can restring you, er, or
loosen your strings, anyway. You know I don't want to use
you, a lot of people might. It isn't even about money, not to
fan cash at you like a peacock tail, but my family *has* money,
now! (*That is, the Knox money is new*) I am complete, I just
want to share my completeness. That has to be better,
doesn't it? (*Pause*) Let's get married. You're my wife elect.

PRISS (*pause*): I'm so mixed up this morning.

HANK: We'd just be dedicating a building that's already finished. (*Pause*) Can't you believe someone could love you,
yourself? You could help me, and I know I can help you!
(*Pause; he tries a breezy joke style*) Besides, I already told
my father we were getting married! He's going to throw us a
party next month! (*This has a dire effect, to* HANK's *horror.*)

PRISS (*blank*): Did you . . . really?

HANK (*panicked*): No. (*Beat*) Yes. (*Beat*) To be honest, yes!

PRISS (*perplexed, amazed, even tender, but suddenly freed*): Oh Hank . . . ! (*Pause*)

(*Blackout.*)

SCENE 9

A nice couch, with HANK *and* PONY *sitting on it. Though friendly, fun and brisk, there is the slightly studied air about this scene that goes with television chat.* HANK *is more flippant and free than most hosts.* PONY *has become surprisingly poised. It isn't immediately obvious this is a TV interview.*

HANK: Your place is really sharp, Tony.

PONY: Thanks.

HANK: Was it impossibly expensive?

PONY: No, just outrageously. I'm still getting settled—I used to live in Hell's Kitchen!

HANK (*playfully*): And what would this neighborhood be? Heaven's Garage? Purgatory's Rec Room?

PONY (*politely game*): Ha! Well, it's called the West Village.

HANK: So these digs are thanks to your movie, which has gone from big to Brobdingnagian at the box office. Tell us about *The Stranger From Earth*, in case anyone out there has been down in a bathysphere for the past month.

PONY: Well, I'm the only human in it, though there's a race of people just like humans. It's very complicated. I have to go to a distant star and claim this inheritance which turns out to be an entire planet.

HANK: Every child's dream. Absolute power.

PONY: They showed me the toys that go with the movie, and it is strange to see my face on a doll. I do hope it turns out to be a sort of mythic thing, though, and not just—what? Marketing.

HANK: So, you're the head of a massive argosy of Merchandise. With all your activities, do you have time for romance? Is there anyone in your life right now?

PONY (*cautiously*): Well, I'm glad to say there is.

HANK: Marriage material? (*What is he thinking of? He's trying to help* PONY's *image.* PONY *laughs uneasily, just as any star would, pinned down prematurely and publicly about a fling*)

PONY (*remarkably skilled*): Well, it's still pretty fresh! And I *am* very busy!

HANK: What do you look for in a woman?

PONY (*unflinching, but hurt*): . . . Honesty?

HANK: Well, love isn't today's problem. (*Now 'begins'*) Tony, you grew up without a father, a challenge millions of kids are facing today. We're going to hear about that, and how your family has coped.

PONY (*taking the ball, ill-advisedly*): Yes. A lot of people who feel like losers might like to know that a lot of people who become winners also feel like losers inside, in fact that's why they become winners—

HANK (*smoothly, but dubious of this non sequitur*): That too, and more. (*He faces front*) Plus Tony's guitar collection! Bla bla bla! (*Laughs*) When we return!

(*Blackout.*)

SCENE 10

PRISS, *in a winter coat, waits on a New York street corner.* HANK *appears, with a bouquet and a wrapped gift.*
HANK: Priss?

PRISS: Hank!

(*They embrace, very fondly. Is this a scheduled rendezvous?*)

HANK: Look at you!

PRISS: Now, I can't do that!

HANK: I'll fill you in: You look great!

PRISS (*echoing his earlier tease*): And I think you . . . are correct!

HANK (*sportingly; he had it coming*): Ha! I deserved that.

PRISS: How's it going?

HANK: Oh, variously, but vigorously. You know me!

PRISS (*wryly*): To an extent! (*To cover any seeming cut*) Did you hear about Mr. Ringer?

HANK: Yes, I'm sorry. Well . . . he can finally meet JFK now! Are you enjoying my job?

PRISS: I'm indifferent. That helps me do good work. And—I'm writing the odd brochure for the Foundation.

HANK: The odd brochure! (*Pause*) And you're seeing that banker, Wayne?

PRISS (*wondering how* HANK *knows*): He's pretty visible, yes.

HANK: And how's that architect, Max? I'm connected to spies, as you know.

PRISS: Well, Max is waning, Wayne is waxing.

HANK: Losers? Winners? Extras? Protagonists?

PRISS: I don't know. All those at once.

HANK: Ah, so.

PRISS: How about you? Anything serious?

HANK: Oh, here and there a pilot episode, but nothing going to series. (*Pause*) So who are you waiting for?

PRISS: Wayne. (*An awkward pause; she's certainly seen the flowers and gift*)

HANK (*anticipating her*): Oh! Allow me a preemptive strike. These flowers are for Rick and his fiancée. Well, bride, if it's past eight. Low-key loft ceremony. Roses. Set of knives.

PRISS: Ahh.

HANK: Kitchen knives. (*Pause*) How's the twin?

PRISS: Teddy got married.

HANK: They're getting married like flies! (*Pause*) Oh look! When did the scaffolding come off that building?

PRISS: They just finished!

HANK: How very big! And new . . . ! Brrr, I feel the wind on my face!

PRISS: Is it that cold?

HANK: I mean from time going by.

PRISS: Ahh.

HANK: Well, I don't want Wayne to beat me up!

PRISS: Oh, Hank. (*Kisses him on the cheek*) I watch you all the time.

HANK: And are you okay?

PRISS: Oh yes . . . (*Pause. She gropes for words*) I finally found my way out of the . . . dark forest . . . of hope!

HANK: Why, you little Zen thing! (*Seeing the 'Don't Walk' flash*)
Oh, I'll catch this light. 'Bye!

PRISS: 'Bye! (*Pause*)

(*Blackout.*)

SCENE 11

Wagnerian Ben Hur consummation music soars. We see PONY,
*his hair wind-swept, alone atop a tiny planet as small as the
Little Prince's, though his expression is all set-jawed and heroic
in his medieval sci–fi finery. He raises an incomprehensible
weapon–cum–sceptre to heaven, while black space sprawls behind. Presumably this is a scene from his hit movie. His tunic
ripples like a flag, and he is the image of the redeeming warrior.
The music soars.*

(*Blackout.*)

SCENE 12

MARGARET *and* MUTT *have set up housekeeping together. He is in
a brown bathrobe, woodworking, wielding a saw and building a
table of biblical simplicity. She sits nearby, dressed in a light
blue robe, her hair wrapped in a light blue towel, serenely tend-
ing a baby chimpanzee. So long as it is unmistakable, a live
chimp or a (more pleasant and convenient) doll may be used.
All are bathed in a shaft of cathedral-style light. Needless to
say, the image is that of the Holy Family.* MARGARET *and* MUTT
*look to each other, smile beatifically, and raise their chimpan-
zee baby playfully on high. The continuing glorious music, that
of* PONY's *quasi-biblical hit movie, rises. Fade out.*

END OF PLAY

AUTHOR'S AFTERWORD

There are many ways to tell one story, just as there are many ways to paint one countryside. With drama, the characters must live and speak for themselves, wittingly or not. A story told in prose has the advantage of an omniscient narrator who can explain the characters' behavior and its implications. The difference is that of Show and Tell.

After writing the outline for Strangers on Earth, *I wanted to interpret it in two ways, as a story and as a play—God's version and the Devil's, perhaps. I hope the useful double lives as novels and plays of Wharton's* The House of Mirth, *Barrie's* Peter Pan *and Steinbeck's* Of Mice and Men *set legitimizing examples against the possible charge of twice cooked cabbage, and of course there are the countless films of novels, novelizations of movies, video games based on cartoons, cereals derived from video games, and dances based on folktales. I include the short story version of* Strangers on Earth *here because it may be of interest to actors, directors or obsessed fans who would like an additional perspective on the play. It appeared in my first collection* Elementary Education, *published by Alfred A. Knopf in 1985.*

Strangers in Town

Hank was an only child, and his parents let him know he was their destiny. They were conservative people, but they liked expansion, so figured it would be best to concentrate their investment in one child. They were Texans, self-made Houstonites who trusted no one, so had to be friendly to everyone, a policy they handed on to Hank by christening him with a nickname. Thanks to vitamins, he grew up tall, which people interpreted as rectitude, and he was oblivious enough to converse effortlessly, which people interpreted as intelligence. His self-confidence sprang from an only child's disbelief in the reality of others, though their belief in him convinced him of his own, so he was habitually ingratiating. When he graduated first in his business school class, his friends gave him a farewell joke trophy, a welded concoction bristling with chrome figures of a bowler, golfer, female swimmer, airplane, and even a dog. The tribute was humorous because his friends thought that would better conceal their jealousy. The farewell was because Hank liked expansion too, so had accepted a job in a New York advertising agency and was in his view ascending there to a broader challenge, to see if people not obliged to be friendly would approve him. It was in New York that he met Priss, Margaret, Pony, and Mutt.

Priss weighed less than her twin brother at birth, and remained in second place as they grew up, since her sober Bostonian parents were old-fashioned and favored boys. She wasn't prissy, but was too shy as a child to forbid the nickname's taking hold. In fact, she was pretty and smart, but doubted both, so people got the impression she was neither. Puberty made her quarrel with her twin and he proceeded to Dartmouth ("Voice Crying in the Desert"), she to Radcliffe ("Truth"). He became a soccer star there, while she wallowed insecurely in the Economics major her parents advised for her security. Her only glory was as Mary Queen of Scots in a house dramatic production: she obediently followed her director's instructions to be commanding, and was. Her only sex life was with a black Kenyan graduate student, an adventure rather than an investment, since she knew from fiction that one doesn't marry the first one. When her parents met him at graduation, she didn't tell them he'd been her boyfriend, and they chose not to assume it. They concentrated instead on loading her things in a rented truck to move her to New York. Her father had arranged a job interview for her at an advertising agency, and, crucial to her decision, her best friend Margaret was joining her in what Margaret called their "kamikaze life pact."

Margaret loved Priss's cleansing blondness and self-effacing plainness, and Priss loved Margaret's spirited blue-collar banter and liberated plainness. Margaret was from Cleveland, not Shaker Heights but depressed, Slavic, broken-down Cleveland itself, so she was guilty of pride. Her family's poverty served her well, because she got a scholarship to Radcliffe, where her love of gossip and the outlandish prompted her to major in Psychology. Her parents were amicably divorced, so she'd been reared to thrive on thorny wisecracks, an inheritance her co-workers feared and enjoyed. She was so sarcastic people could guess she was a virgin. When she decided to move to New York after graduation to study language acquisition in apes with a Columbia professor, her friends at the lab gave her a fully assembled Visible Woman and a signed mash note from King Kong. She was also the cause of wit in others, which was what Mutt would love in her.

Mutt pretended to be stupid for the sake of his Italian father, and shiftless so his Irish mother could fulfill herself by waiting on him. He was a healthy ten-pounder, christened Matthew and reared in South Boston, where it was to his social advantage to slouch and feign worthlessness. He was a sensation as Frank Sinatra one Halloween, and as a result let traces of the impersonation govern him thereafter. He bypassed college as a gesture of solidarity with his overage hoodlum brothers. Actually, he was a good carpenter and discovered women would sleep with him if he built them bookcases or tables. Eventually, their recommendations led to his doing woodwork for strangers. He'd done some repair work for Priss's father and was recommended by him to fix up Priss and Margaret's New York apartment. He had a van and friends in an NYU fraternity he could stay with, so he took the job. That's when he met Margaret and Priss, and Hank and Pony.

Pony (a nickname he coined and desperately promoted himself) was born in Salt Lake City, premature and underweight, disadvantages he exploited to get his way over his three elder sisters and mother. His father, in observance of the Mormon motto of Industry, had died of a heart attack (he was a secret coffee drinker) when Pony was two years old. As a result, his sisters and mother spoiled him, which made him underestimate feminine approval and long for masculine affirmation. He grew up nice-looking in a commercial Mormon way, but his height (five foot four) reduced him to cute. Like many children who are overindulged and sense it, he was self-involved and self-doubtful simultaneously, which—coupled with a scrupulous lack of briefing on the facts of life—ultimately expressed itself as homosexuality. He was not smart, which went undetected in his set, but he was limber and could play the guitar, which led him to sing morale-boosters for his church youth gatherings, as compensation for his secret evil and as a means to exhibit himself. Since college can be considered superfluous for guitar players, he chose to take a bus to New York and be discovered. It was ill-considered but that didn't mean it had to be ill-fated.

Once at Ringer and Bellman (the ad agency), Hank was quickly distinguished as a leader, since he made inconsequential decisions without hesitation. Even the personnel director asked Hank whom he liked among job applicants. When Priss was interviewed, Hank liked her in the corridor and gave his boss the go-ahead. Priss had canceled her first interview because she became ill over it, and concentrated on watching Mutt fix up the new apartment, though Margaret warned her, "Food before nest." The second scheduled interview went smoothly, since her father had been promised she would get the job, and her interviewer had decided to be friendly to her to entertain himself. The only flub that haunted her was her improvised confession that she'd wished she'd majored in Psychology, for advertising's sake, and didn't know why she hadn't majored in Psychology, but if she had perhaps she could explain why she hadn't. She got the job.

Margaret had sustained Priss through her counterfeit illness with jokes about resenting her helplessness, and also managed Mutt, who, finding his employers helpless, had great fun by teasing them and behaving like a friendly gorilla: it took him a month to do a two-week job. Sleeping in a partly painted apartment by shifting from room to room depressed Priss, whose people were not nomadic, so Margaret had to rally for them both, especially to check Mutt's unwitting sexual displays. It was the longest audition Mutt had ever had.

Pony and his secretly acquired mirrored sunglasses arrived at Port Authority at twilight. He stepped from his bus into the chaser lights, maniac evangelists, erotica stands, and prerecorded church bells of Times Square. A prostitute he politely refused taunted him for being gay, which he took as a sign that city dwellers see through everything remorselessly. Unnerved, he stuck to his YMCA room, secretly suspecting there might be a cheaper place to stay, eating cookies he kept in the provided dresser, and writing clumsy guitar ballads about being cooped up in a room. His endless practicing was poignant, but his songs were not. Finally he felt shrewd by buying and scanning the listed casting calls in the trade papers. He needed actor's photos, but cut up his posed family picture for the first tryout he resolved to brave.

Told he was ineligible for the television commercial role he applied for, he took his undersize trapezoidal photo and handwritten credits to the agency involved, assuming they would think of him next time. As it happened, Hank saw Pony trying to convince Priss, who was filling in for the receptionist, to keep the picture, though she protested that they did no casting there. Pony demonstrated his Elvis—you could tell it was Elvis because the song was "Blue Suede Shoes"—though softly, since he knew enough not to make a scene. Hank was entertained, since Texans love odd anecdotes, and felt beholden to Pony after retelling the scene several times, so got him called for a caffeine-free cola commercial requiring nonthreatening rambunction. Pony got the job.

Priss began her job before Margaret's summer vacation ended (her professor summered in the jungle), so Margaret found herself alone with Mutt. He had established a courtship with both girls as a safe joke, but circumstances found him inviting Margaret to visit him at his adoptive fraternity sometime. She was lonely—Priss had met Hank and was busy conjecturing—and unconsciously frightened by her building's creepy superintendent, whose vague sexual bids had turned to sullen unavailability when they were overlooked. Half interested and half frightened of future plumbing problems, she visited Mutt, at his specifically vague suggestion, unexpectedly, the following night. She found him flipping rude jokes about a porno video he and some sophomores were screening. She had respected his lowness but this she felt called for anger on principle, since no graceful date could follow anyway. Luckily, he had only one more day's work on the Casa Kamikaze, as Margaret called it. They parted badly, which planted the sensation of a romance in them.

Hank took Priss on an Upper West Side date: cartoons at the Thalia, where an audience of adults laughed at a Thirties Looney Tune of premarital violence between two pigs. Despite this potential damper, they managed to align via Chinese food, and had sex at Hank's apartment. Since both were new in New York they assumed it was the polite standard. They got along so well Hank decided it was better she not spend the night. They parted vaguely, which, coupled with the August humidity, planted the sensation of a romance in them.

Pony, and a group of bikini-clad adults who played adolescents professionally, filmed the commercial, circling the Statue of Liberty on a tugboat spruced up for the occasion, dancing with well-rehearsed abandon and waving bottles of Yes at the westward horizon. After hours, the wholesome-looking cast introduced Pony to cocaine, pot, and overly social drinking. He had been carefully reared, so had no ready resistance. He became known as Mister Twist and Shout, but only after a certain point in the evening. Hank appeared at the shooting several times, always in the morning, so Pony associated him with paternal strength and hard work. Hank was automatically encouraging to Pony, which planted the sensation of a romance in Pony.

Mutt and Margaret had a difficult phone call, since he was helpless when his Frank Sinatra act was inappropriate. Her insults, however, convinced him she believed in his better self. Powered by inanition, he remained in town and got a job as a bicycle messenger. Since his co-workers were all uneducated black teenagers, he took this as a sign of his savvy and validity. Margaret was attracted to Mutt—he was big, dumb, and sexy, like the universe—but feared his good temper and interest in her proved he had no ambition. Then, in the tradition of expanding frustration, her impending employer was accused of falsifying data. Much had been made of his spectacular report that a chimp he had trained to speak sign language had, in a moment of anger, spontaneously combined the symbols for excrement and rotten food with the sign for the professor's name. A colleague claimed this was a fiction for publicity, and demanded duplication of results. The controversy suspended Margaret's beginning work, and the sensation of joblessness in New York opened beneath her.

Priss assumed Hank could never love her, and subtly encouraged him to vindicate her belief. Actually, he assumed he loved Priss, since he felt aimlessly comfortable with her apparent self-sufficiency. Before he could tell her, though, he was sent on a publicity tour as the sudden co-author of a book. His boss had moonlighted a hopeful self-help best-seller called *You Can Make Them Like You*, but was so grating and ugly his publishers felt a front man was needed for top talk-show impact. Hank was so appealing his boss returned to work and let him complete the tour himself, and the book did very well, further proof to Priss that Hank's life was too full to add her. She was lonely because she lacked even herself.

Pony projected his movie fantasies of rescue on the screen of Hank's white shirts, and dogged him with the imperviousness of the gauche among the gracious. His swizzle of a Yes was used to cap the commercial, and he got more ad work; his inner confusion gave him an expression directors felt an audience could relate to. He next played an older brother bested by his toddler competitor's fleet of toy trucks, and then the person least likely to understand computers finally understanding one. He joined a guild and got an agent, in exchange for which God-sent bribe he reflexively volunteered celibacy, another of the secret scandals of show business. However, his deal with God allowed him drugs and alcohol.

Priss and Margaret's spurned super implied he knew it was they who had spray-painted obscenities on their elevator walls, since Priss and Margaret were the youngest residents, and he didn't know about Radcliffe. This eerie fillip roused them to organize a Labor Day weekend escape. They rented a car, just like Manhattan adults, who unlike their parents have casual relations with many cars rather than buy one and take care of parking. Priss invited Hank, whose compulsive courtesy forced him to invite Pony, who was standing in Hank's office when Priss phoned. Pony was to balance the picture, and hence Margaret's pride, Hank later realized he had reasoned.

The weekend was a rout of skew interests; without surrounding noise, New York dementia enters bold relief. On the drive up, Pony tried to break the rented-car ice by leading the singing of rounds, unaware it maddened his companions. "All things shall perish from under the sky, Music alone shall live, never to die" was his last gambit as they sighted Priss's family's Cape Cod beach house. Mutt, wet from a swim, was waiting on the porch when they arrived. He had come uninvited and unwelcome as a heroic gesture, and Margaret lambasted him, though with a rubber-tipped pitchfork, since she was secretly riveted by his rudeness for love's sake. Pony was disappointed by the existence of Priss, but was guiltily sunny to her. His attentions to her made Priss sense he was her rival, though she was impressed with the grown-up feeling of it. Margaret had decided not to like Hank, as a safety balance for infatuated Priss's sake, and was stymied by his charm when she finally spent time with him. Mutt's ironic boorishness confused literal-minded Pony, and Pony's loud-mouthed inhibitedness made the group inwardly reckon him a tormented deputy of the Born Again, even though he'd barely been born once. Hank vaguely sensed the disparities, but believed it was kindest not to acknowledge trouble until necessary, so felt that entitled him not to consider it.

Pony, gladdened by wine, sang around the fire, which made Priss and Hank begin to glaze, and Mutt led Margaret out for a walk when Pony took a break to deliver patter between songs.

On the moonlit beach, Margaret remembered a chaos even more basic than Cleveland. She commented on the scuttling and striving of the crabs and beached fish, and that the tides of the ocean and of animal appetite expressed the inexorable pulsation and impinging gravities of the subparticles of the Big Bang. Mutt tenderly agreed, and they made love. He was surprised by her virginity, and that flattered her. It was awkward, but she didn't know enough to resent the gritty sand, and he found it an exotic change from the convenient. Afterward, she wondered aloud if there were a word for happy and sad at once. Mutt suggested sappy.

Hank and Priss also excused themselves from Pony and retired to make love, but secreted in and surrounded by civilization, in the form of a room with a secure door. Believing he didn't love her made Priss cherish their sex. Wishing to be helpful, Hank said he loved her. After he fell asleep, Priss wondered what was taking the inevitable crisis.

Mutt and Margaret returned to find Pony passed out on the porch, having consoled himself into stupefaction. They put him to bed and proceeded to theirs warm with their own charity. Just at dawn, sleepless Priss took a walk on the beach, tense with the chilly air and waves, but borne up by their authoritative recommendation of acceptance. She had just decided to accept when she saw a young couple on an unsaddled horse ride by through the surf's edge, man and woman naked to the waist, their bare legs knit like twins in a womb. Priss winced at its preposterously standard beauty. Back at the house she put on coffee, and when Margaret emerged, announced to her she was going to get psychiatric help. Margaret, having majored in Psychology, discouraged her, but primarily to downplay Priss's problems and proceed to outline her own new hopes and imaginings. Sexual knowledge had shattered Margaret's worldliness.

Back in the city, Pony decided to spurn Hank as punishment for being unaware of him. Happily for him, Pony was next cast in a movie, *The Stranger from Earth*, a low-budget fantasy in which he starred as the lovable laird of a desert-island-sized asteroid, ultimately master to a blue-skinned beauty and, after the film, the figurehead of a massive merchandising argosy. He went to Hollywood and gave up drinking, and in exchange at last he could have all the sex he wanted. He didn't feel people saw through him out there.

Hank shivered when Pony retracted his approval, since it was an unfamiliar feeling, and again later when Pony's hit movie made the loss seem more substantial. Priss receded from Hank as well, at first to test his interest but finally to keep her restored breathing regular.

Hank might have tried to keep her, but he felt bullied when he interpreted her request for a separation as a request for marriage, so had to resist it by surrendering to it. Eventually, he left the agency and became a talk-show host, a beloved short-term listener, applauded on videotapes he could save. His guests on *Success Talk* were famous unmarried couples and concocted teen stars who recited with conceited frankness how they managed careers and real identities. To their undemanding narcissism Hank turned the one-way mirror of his eyes and reassured them they existed. At last he overcame his many advantages, and found a verifiable reality.

Priss went to a psychiatrist several times, but his insidious silence so reminded her of her superintendent she asked not to continue with him. He forbade it, since she had so far to go, but for once she declined sponsorship and left his office. He yelled after her that she would never be free. However, as she discovered the competence born of indifference, she was promoted at Ringer and Bellman and was often asked out. Her Kenyan ex-boyfriend, now engaged, passed through New York and they slept together, expecting nothing from it. It was the best sex she'd ever had. At last she found her way out of the dark forest of hope.

Mutt's messenger service decided to upgrade its image and fired all its employees but Mutt, which was a blow to his self-respect. His bosses' plan was to recast themselves as Preppin' Fetchit, and provide a white adult in Brooks Brothers clothes to run any client's errands. It was a great success, but without Mutt, who regarded neckties as unmasculine. Luckily, the next trapeze arrived before he could tumble: in the tradition of expanding good fortune, he lucked into a loft that was unreasonably rather than impossibly overpriced, and there built furniture on commission for his neighbors' friends. Margaret moved in with him. At last he transcended his fraternal urge to underreach himself.

Margaret's job came through when her boss was cleared, at least inasmuch as his accuser was discovered to have fabricated many of the most horrifying anecdotes in his famous book on the effects of overcrowding on rats. Margaret was a hit with staff and apes alike, and Mutt often joined her at the lab to watch admiringly as she trained a young chimp to sign. They would have made a lovely scene, if anyone had seen them: the virtual virgin, her carpenter husband, their miraculous child. At last Margaret could believe in modern family life.